# Pilgrims to the Wild

# Pilgrims to the Wild

Everett Ruess
Henry David Thoreau
John Muir
Clarence King
Mary Austin

John P. O'Grady

University of Utah Press
Salt Lake City

∞ This symbol indicates books printed on paper that meets the mini-mum requirements of American National Standard for Information Ser-vices—Permanence of Paper for Printed Library Materials, ANSI A39.38–1984.

Library of Congress Cataloging-in-Publication Data

O'Grady, John P., 1958–
    Pilgrims to the wild : Everett Ruess, Henry David Thoreau, John
Muir, Clarence King, Mary Austin / by John P. O'Grady.
        p.   cm.
    Includes bibliographical references and index.
    ISBN 0–87480–412–4 (alk. paper)
    1. American prose literature—History and criticism.
    2.  Naturalists—United States—Biography—History and criticism.
    3.  Authors, American—Biography—History and criticism.
    4.  Wilderness areas—United States—Historiography.   5.  Natural
history—United States—Historiography.   6.  Wilderness areas in
literature.   7.  Nature in literature.   I.  Title.
    PS163.018   1993
    818' .08—dc20                                                    92-29783
                                                                        CIP

# Contents

Space reaches out from us and translates the world.
— Rainer Maria Rilke

# Preface

*The time and my intents are savage-wild,*
*More fierce and inexorable by far*
*Than empty tigers or raring sea.*
                              —Romeo and Juliet (*V:iii 37–39*)

This preface should have been written atop a mountain. I tried. Before I wrote the bulk of this book, I climbed Koip Peak, in the Yosemite High Sierra, late one dark afternoon in August 1990, outfitted with notebook and good intentions, but an immense thunderstorm—outstanding disturbance—interrupted my jottings, routing me from the peak in a panic of self-preservation. Yosemite National Park was set afire, I almost perished from hypothermia, and that preface was never completed. It's just as well. The word *preface* itself is a contradiction—literally a "speaking before"—and, as every reader knows, the preface is the final bit of book indited. Herein lies an austere beauty: The last written shall be the first read. The beginning is the ending.

Koip Peak offered me no words. A mountain needs no preface, requires no apology, no explanation. So I turn instead to literature, to a poet who lived his most significant days beyond the mountains. In the late 1930s, Kenneth Rexroth composed a book-length manuscript entitled "Camping in the Western Mountains." Written under the auspices of the Federal Writers Project, the book for some reason never saw publication. Perhaps it was ahead of its time—or maybe just too idiosyncratic, too ornery, to have found a market. In any case, this manuscript, yellowed and languishing now in a prosaic library, provides a thorough introduction to all aspects of backcountry camping as it was understood at the time; its subjects range from sleeping-bag construction to the arcana of equine constipation. Although he clearly intended his book to be a technical self-help manual for the outdoor enthusiast, Rexroth, the poet-litterateur-anarchist could not refrain from interjecting his own unmistakable voice into the treatise and, in so doing, revealing his love for the subject matter.

Toward the end of the manuscript, he suggests a number of books that might be useful to readers unfamiliar with the "philosophy" of roughing it. He says, "There are books that have nothing to do with camping, and less to do with the Western mountains, that are valuable preparations for a camping trip."[1] Rexroth recommends that the novice camper stuff a remarkable assortment of books into the pack: Izaak Walton's *The Compleat Angler*, Gilbert White's *The Natural History of Selbourne*, and—most remarkable of all—John Bunyan's *The Pilgrim's Progress*. Although the first two books are tangentially related to outdoor pursuits, the backpacking reader may wonder why Rexroth declares Bunyan's work to be among "the three best manuals for camping and woodcraft that will ever be written." Lofty praise indeed, even exaggerated, but Rexroth's words are insightful, providing us with a point of departure: The pilgrim is a spiritual bushwhacker. Or to phrase it in more anthropological terms: "A pilgrim is one who divests himself of the mundane concomitants of religion . . . to confront, in a special 'far' milieu, the basic elements and structures of his faith in their unshielded, virgin radiance" (Victor and Edith Turner 15).[2]

*Pilgrims to the Wild* is a series of meditations on literary journeys to "the wild," what I call secular pilgrimages. Though Bunyan's pilgrim traveled only with his soul, tracking his bliss into heavenly oblivion, the five figures I will be following traveled in real places, with their bodies as well as their souls. Furthermore, Bunyan's Christian violated the cardinal rule of pilgrimage: He didn't come home. The pilgrim, by definition, is supposed to return to his formerly mundane existence, his community, in a state of spiritual enlightenment. In this sense, Bunyan's Christian is no pilgrim at all, but a traitor to his community. Sometimes this also happens, as we

---

1. The manuscript is housed in the Special Collections of the Doheny Library at the University of Southern California.

2. The Turners claim that "pilgrimage has been surprisingly neglected by historians and social scientists. But perhaps it has merely shared in the general disregard of the liminal and marginal phenomena of social processes and cultural dynamics by those intent either upon the description and classification of orderly institutionalized 'facts' or upon the establishment of the 'historicity' of prestigious, unrepeated events" (1).

shall see in the case of Everett Ruess, among travelers who venture into the wild. But if one is a writer—that is, one whose fundamental role within the community is to communicate to that community—this pilgrim must return, even if only through the medium of the written word.

In approaching the varied terrain covered by my pilgrims to the wild, I do not ask, "What are these texts about?" but, rather, "What is happening here—and to whom?" I am less interested in making arguments than in following trails and sometimes leaving those trails for a cross-country excursion. Friends who have traveled with me through the California wildlands occasionally complain of my propensity for free and not-so-easy wandering, where the way is seldom clear; they are particularly peeved when we come back covered with horrendous mementos of poison oak, a plant the Pomo Indians called *Ma-tu-ya-ho*, "the southern fire doctor." The itch we receive from this renegade member of the sumac family offers nothing to intellection, but it does stick with us, a tangible mark of our journey, for weeks afterward. Scratch, scratch, scratch.

Each of my pilgrims to the wild—Henry David Thoreau, John Muir, Clarence King, Mary Hunter Austin, and Everett Ruess—is a writer who documents the crossing of thresholds. The fundamental assumption I employ—call it a perception—is that "the wild" is erotic space, and the pilgrimages I am concerned with are journeys through that space. A caution here: By identifying the wild as "erotic space," I by no means intend to be reductionist, but just the opposite—which has its own risks. In my various meditations, I frequently resort to use of the word *desire*, but I take great pains to show the special way(s) in which I use this word. It is slippery. Yes. Perhaps I should have settled for a term like the Taoist *Wu-yü*, which has a meaning akin to "the absence of material desires," or what David L. Hall has translated as "objectless desire," a seemingly odd locution but perhaps more effective. "The claim here is that enjoyments are possible without the demand that one define, possess, or control the occasion of one's enjoyment" (Callicott 109). The danger in relying so heavily on a single word to convey one's meaning is that the meaning finally disappears under the definition. It is this moment of disappearance that—more than any-

thing else—intrigues me. I seek it in the writings of all my pilgrims.

That I have chosen the lives and works of five particular American writers should not be interpreted as a gesture of "canon forma-
tion," the identification of a core of literary texts that stakes out a
tradition. I am not interested in canons, but in affinities. With the
exception of Everett Ruess (and it is because of his constant "exception" that I begin my meditations with him), all of my pilgrims
to the wild belong to the tradition of American nature writing, all
have been included in the recent *Norton Book of Nature Writing*.
Rather than an addition to the burgeoning body of critical inquiry
directed toward nature writing, *Pilgrims to the Wild* is a contribution
to the study of American spiritual autobiography. All of these writers share a lineage with William Bradford, Jonathan Edwards, Eliz-
abeth Ashbridge, and John Woolman. In this sense, *Pilgrims to the
Wild* is concerned with individual perception and psychological
transformation—not historical materialism or sociological analysis,
which in themselves could generate a worthy academic exposition,
but not the book I have written.

The literary scholar too often resembles Bunyan's Christian,
hauling an awkward bundle of "stuff" that hinders progress. The
scholar's bundle is stuffed with words. *Pilgrims to the Wild* is my
bundle. Yet perseverance furthers. When it comes to my writerly
intentions, I think of the lines from Bunyan's own Preface (which
he called an "Apology"): "This book will make a traveller of thee."
Such is my hope. Though fearing the reproach of excessiveness, I
indulge in bricolage, working with ideas at hand, no matter how
far afield in space and time their respective provenances may lie.
This approach can be messy. I assume the repeatability of ideas and
events across cultures and over time, and that the boundaries fashioned to separate these ideas and events are subject to dissolution.
Thus, the thirteenth-century Japanese philosopher Dogen and the
nineteenth-century American Thoreau are mutually illuminating.
In taking this approach, I realize that I confront the margins of ac-
ceptable scholarship: My critical practice puts me right on the
limen, and perhaps—wayward scholar that I am—I occasionally
step too far. But I have been out gathering, and this is what I have
brought back.

# Acknowledgments

If life is a pilgrimage, then I have been blessed with a host of companions along the way, without whose help my progress would have been halted long ago. I would like to acknowledge: my parents, Joseph and Muriel O'Grady; my brothers, Brian and Peter; my extended family, Corinne, Stephanie, and Christine; my many friends, including Bill Alsup, Scott Anchors, Eric Beckwitt, Steve Beckwitt, Paula Bennett, Josie Bloomfield, Wolfgang Breidenstein, Cheryll Burgess, Nancy Burkhalter, Deidre Busacca, Greg Carr, Ed Castellini, Michael P. Cohen, Terry Cronin, Greg Downing, Marilyn Emerick, Harold Fromm, Anne Goldman, Charles Greenhalgh, Betsy Hilbert, Jonathan Howland, Andrew Kirk, Tiina Kirss, Carole Koda, Steve Kubacki, Nancy Louk-Murphy, Tim Lyons, Jody McCarthy, Nash Mayfield, Dale Metcalfe, Kem Miller, Ted Murphy, Alice Norton, Joan O'Connell, Janet Papale, Paul Puccio, Sondra Reid, Joan Reiss, Eric Paul Shaffer, Nancy Sisko, Scott Slovic, Susan Small, Sabine Stoll Smith, Sanford Smith, Dirk Stratton, Gary Taylor, Kim Takayama, Barbara Taylor, James Taylor III, Jan VanStavern, Paul Vatalaro, Blake Voss, Joyce Wade, Jennifer Westphal, Michael Westphal, Helena Whalen-Bridge, and John Whalen-Bridge. I must also acknowledge the outstanding teachers and mentors I have had: Tony Brinkley, Peter Dale, T. Jeff Evans, Ted Foin, Daniel Fraustino, Burton Hatlen, Stephen King, Michael P. Kramer, Michael Kudish, Marijane Osborn, K. Ludwig Pfeiffer, Winfried Schleiner, and Michael L. Smith. A special thanks to David Robertson and Gary Snyder. A Regents Fellowship from the University of California, Davis, granted me a year of necessary research and wandering. Also, this book would not have been the book that it is were it not for the support of the Huntington

Library, as well as the Special Collections staffs at the University of Southern California, the University of Arizona, and the University of New Mexico. Finally, I would like to pay a tribute to the Livingston Public Library in Livingston, New Jersey: for helping me read my way out of the suburbs.

# Abbreviations

CLB—Austin, Mary. *Stories from the Country of Lost Borders.*
Corr—Thoreau, H. D. *The Correspondence of Henry David Thoreau.*
EH—Austin, Mary. *Earth Horizon.*
FS—Muir, John. *My First Summer in the Sierra.*
HEH—Henry E. Huntington Library, San Marino, California.
J—Thoreau, H. D. *The Journal of Henry David Thoreau.*
JOM—Muir, John. *John of the Mountains.*
LF—Muir, John. *Letters to a Friend.*
TMW—Muir, John. *A Thousand-Mile Walk to the Gulf.*

# ONE

# The Story of Everett Ruess

*"Longing, we say, because desire is full of endless distances."*
—Robert Hass, "Meditation at Lagunitas"

"Nemo." No one. Thus begins and ends what is by a certain standard the most successful bit of nature writing ever attempted by an American. The Word can come no closer to the utterly wild. Its author, twenty-year-old Everett Ruess, called a "vagabond for beauty," disappeared in November of 1934, dissolving in an unwitnessed performance (if we are to believe the story) from the remote Utah canyonlands south and east of Escalante, shortly after inscribing his text, Anasazi-like, into the inscrutable sandstone. An extensive search in the spring of 1935, involving citizens from throughout the state of Utah as well as Navajo "trackers" from the other side of the Colorado, recovered only the artist's two burros, penned into an isolated canyon, hungry but still healthy after four months of abandonment. Of Ruess himself, of his abandon, of his longing, the only traces uncovered by the search parties were some footprints, leading in no particular direction, and some scratchings on the rock—what amounted to his petroglyph:

NEMO
1934

It remains a remarkable contribution to American nature writing. Everett Ruess, another teenager in search of himself, was overwhelmed by desire, a romantic who escaped the city, a writer who escaped writing, an artist who, before he ever became known, became unknown. Everett Ruess, the one who walked away. Everett Ruess, the escapee. But he would not get far—even he could not escape the trammel of myth; ghosts too are impounded, by the terrain they haunt.

Ruess was born in Oakland, California, on March 28, 1914. His mother, Stella Knight Ruess, a painter and poet, was a "follower of a philosophy typified by the great dancer Isadora Duncan, that

1

women should freely express their idealistic and romantic inclina-
tions and, above all, should determine their own destinies" (Rusho
4). She bestowed upon the family a motto, one that amounted to
an artistic credo: "Glorify The Hour." Christopher Ruess, Everett's
father, was of like mind. Harvard Divinity School graduate, proba-
tion officer, Unitarian minister, he was once asked by his son: "Is
there any fulfillment that endures as such, besides death?" Christopher Ruess's response: "I doubt if death fulfills. It seems to end but
I doubt that it ends much. Not one's influence or the influence of
one's work. Perhaps even the echoes of your voice may go on forever. Some instrument might pick them up years or ages hence.
Beauty is an ultimate fulfillment, as is Goodness, as is Truth. These
are ends in themselves, and are for the sake of life. Many things are
worthwhile that are not enduring. Eternity is just made of todays.
Glorify the hour" (123). Resplendent in Emersonian haze, the
story of Everett Ruess acquires an inevitability, a certain fate.

For the first fourteen years of his life, Ruess's family engaged in
chronic migrations, from Oakland to Fresno to Los Angeles to
Massachusetts to New York to Indiana, before settling finally in
the most unsettled of places, Hollywood, California. A mutual pursuit of beauty united them; nomadism was a family affair. Despite
these clannish peregrinations, Everett, at the age of twelve, was
able to attend weekly classes at the Chicago Art Institute, and—
when finally enrolled in Hollywood High School—took classes at
the Otis Art School. Prior to his last semester, he hitchhiked up
the California coast past Big Sur, where he spent two months in-
gratiating himself, or so he believed, among the artists in Carmel,
including the photographer Edward Weston.

From his letters, it is clear that Ruess's discovery of this artistic
community was more fortuitous than it was planned. To his
mother, he reported: "When I got back in town I went to Edward
Weston's studio and made friends with him. A man who gave me a
ride near Morro Bay had told me about him" (12). Weston was
perhaps charmed by such naiveté, but it is unlikely that he or any
of the other artists spent a great deal of time in fostering this odd
young man. Instead, Ruess spent long days wandering along that
then-lonely edge of North America, up and down canyon slopes,
through coastal scrub, woodland valleys of oak, and the southern-

most extension of the redwood forest, making his sketches, painting the occasional watercolor, and writing poems—none of which caught the attention, positive or negative, of any of the established Carmel artists. Perhaps he spent too much time outdoors, losing himself in space while the others were busy organizing it. His idea of art could not be contained within the walls of the studio. "I made a water color under the most difficult conditions I have yet endured," he writes to his mother, describing an attempt he made to paint while on a wild stretch of beach. "The wind blew sand into my paint and on my picture all the time I was painting. The sand is still stuck to the picture, and produced an interesting effect, but I don't think there will be much color left on the picture when the sand comes off" (19). The blur in his perception between subject and object is straightaway established; representation is already problematic. Ruess, it would seem, was always an extremist.

Even so, he remained in Carmel for some time because he was in search of a mentor—Weston a magnetic possibility. The photographer, unfortunately, simply did not have the time to indulge young Ruess. Weston—an artist, not a teacher—once wrote to Ansel Adams: "You are absolutely right about keeping remote. . . . Our kind of work cannot be done on 'main street.' . . . I am not anti-social; I have a deep affection for my friends and family, feel deeply for suffering humanity (also for suffering animals) but at times I have a desperate need to be absolutely alone" (Enyeart 11). Though it is impossible to determine exactly what effect such a strong, artistic personality might have had on Ruess, we can surmise some affinity between their creative temperaments—but we should keep in mind that Ruess at this time was only sixteen years old. Weston was a disciplined, working professional, an artist with a hankering for solitude; Ruess was a sensitive, restless adolescent who may have mistaken the artist's practiced accomplishment as license for eccentricity and egoistic posturing. Poetic sensibility fueled Ruess, until he finally disappeared four years later in an extravagant pilgrimage to the wild. As a counter example to this, in the various forms of Buddhism that stress the importance of finding an appropriate teacher, the practice of pilgrimage was reserved for attained and well-settled monks—the journey regarded as the flowering of a rigorous self-discipline. Everett Ruess never found his guide.

His pursuit of beauty, undisciplined as it was, nevertheless became a journey toward the self. Although he brings his sketchbook with him, it is not for art he seeks "the Wild," but for a sense of his identity. This pilgrim seeks solitude, resorting to lonely, "unspoiled" places where he may say he communes with nature but, in actuality, seeks communion with what Buddhists call the Original Self. "There is a splendid freedom in solitude," Ruess writes from a remote place, "and after all, it is for solitude that I go to the mountains and deserts, not for companionship. In solitude I can bare my soul to the mountains unabashed. I can work or think, act or recline at my whim, and nothing stands between me and the Wild" (Rusho 143). The next place we find him, in August of that same summer, is Yosemite National Park, writing a letter at the conclusion of a backcountry pilgrimage that took him from the Yosemite Valley to Glen Aulin to Lake Tenaya, over Cloud's Rest, down past Nevada and Vernal Falls, and back to Yosemite Valley again. He describes, to his family, his return to civilization: "The whole atmosphere was one of anti-climax. I was returning from the mountains and solitude to the valley, and the noisy, uninitiated tourists, and eventually to the city and its sordid buildings and business places" (23).

Ruess's desire for solitude must not be mistaken for misanthropy. As was the case with Weston, and indeed with many articulate seekers and fashioners of the self, this desire to be alone is ultimately superseded by a longing for a community of friends. "It is true," Ruess writes to one friend, "that I can be happy alone and many times I've felt relieved to be in solitude. I look forward to my trip tomorrow because it will take me into solitude again. But a real friend is not an intrusion" (57). To his father he remarks: "A friend is a wonderful treasure" (53). His letters are saturated with a yearning for community, for "communitas," which Victor and Edith Turner define as the "undifferentiated, egalitarian, direct, extant, nonrational, existential, I-Thou (in Buber's sense)" bonding between human beings (250). From Chinle, Arizona, he tells his brother: "The thing I miss, here as elsewhere, is intelligent companionship. Then too, it seems wrong that people should mean so little to one another. This certainly could be a glorious world. Neglected opportunities are piled sky-high. I have not met any intelligent girls out here" (Rusho 77). If solitude represents the ebb of desire, communitas represents its flow.

Like many misinterpreted interpreters of the wild, Everett Ruess was no antisocial hermit. His pilgrimage, his wandering throughout the Southwest, was as much a search for community as it was for beauty—the two are synonymous. The pilgrim engaged in movement, when approaching the boundary of the known, senses peripherality in the experience of communitas, an "unmediated communication, even communion between definite and determinate identities" (Victor and Edith Turner 250). Here, the pilgrim fronts the edge of the individual self, the loosening selvage of the ego. Among writers who take the wild as their subject, the recurring insight is that the wild within is inseparable from the wild without: self and other become meaningless distinctions. The word *pilgrim* itself suggests as much. Derived from an Indo-European root (*ghedh-*) meaning "to unite, join, fit," it flourishes in modern English as the words *good, gad, gather,* and *together.* Thus, it can be said that the pilgrim is a gatherer, and "to gather together" is a pleonasm that means "good." An Old Germanic cognate (*gaduri-*) translates as "in a body"; thus even when conducted alone, pilgrimage always embodies a notion of the pilgrim's community.

Ruess returned to Los Angeles for the autumn of 1930, just long enough to finish his last term in school, but resumed his wanderings by February of 1931. Although, at his father's urging, he did attend one semester at UCLA, he would remain a "vagabond" for the remainder of his known days. During the next three years, he would explore, on foot and by horse or burro, Monument Valley, Canyon de Chelly, the San Francisco Peaks, the Grand Canyon, the Utah canyonlands, Mesa Verde, Navajo land, Hopi villages—the entire country now designated by the tourist industry as the "Four Corners Region." His letters teem with reference to the many people he met, Indian and white—some of whom he befriended; some for whom he'd work (usually to obtain board); some of whom he would merely pass on the road or trail, acknowledging them simply as fellow travelers, the swelling unfortunates of the Great Depression, destination of no consequence. On December

13, 1933, he writes from San Francisco to his father: "A year ago my Communist friends were firing it at me when I told them that beauty and friendship were all I asked of life. I am not unconcerned with the crisis of our civilization, but the way of the agitator, the social leader, and the politician is not my way. It is not in my nature to deal with masses of people and be an organizer, and I don't propose to make any fundamental changes in my nature. I couldn't change that anyway" (Rusho 124). For all his adolescent excess, Ruess did possess the intuitive sense to pursue his own way of being in the world.

One gets the sense from reading his letters that although the land is vast, rugged, and a seemingly inhospitable desert, it is not deserted of human beings; they are there, passing through, both in time present and time past: now a hobo, now an Anasazi ghost, now a rancher, now an archaeologist, now a Navajo, now a Hollywood film crew. There is human commerce, but relations are unfixed, always temporary, and the style of human existence in these complex, arid lands is that of contingent circulation, a sort of aimless gadding. Life in such a place, with its unpredictable environment and resultant human vagrancy, is best described as unstable, but it is more germane to say that such life can be outright dangerous. This was the fraying edge of American society, the stage for the "Wild West," traversed by dispossessed natives, fortune hunters, cattle rustlers, outlaws, movie companies, and tourists—pilgrims all.

When moments of human companionship erupt upon this scene, they are sudden, unexpected, and register as gifts upon the observant Everett Ruess. He writes from the Grand Canyon: "Many times I have been broke. I was broke yesterday, and I met another young chap who was all but broke. He turned out to be a very likeable and intelligent person. I showed him about the canyon and gave him the first good meal he'd had in a long time. I arranged so that he had a good night's sleep. He left home in order not to handicap his family financially" (61). This encounter with an "intelligent" vagabond underscores Ruess's longing for human community. Wanderers such as this "young chap" are "broke" financially, but so too in spirit—aimless desperation characterizes their peregrinations, though here and there a chance encounter flowers into communitas, renewing the spirit.

As much as Ruess faced the task of making sense of his artistic aspirations and yearning for community, these preoccupations were complicated and sometimes supplanted by hormones—sexual desire, the longing to touch and be touched by the flesh of another human body, to find an "intelligent girl." Indeed, if it is possible for some humans in their most analytic moments to unravel the coils of desire that are mind and body, Ruess was not one of them.

Of his amorous adventures, a glimmer of their energy—joyful, embarrassing, wildly unstable—is shunted to us through the supple decay of his letters. This epistolary record flickers in moments of intimacy with a woman named Frances, whom he met in San Francisco during his six-month sojourn there in the winter of 1933–1934. Little survives of her identity, save what lingers in these letters:

> December 14 [1933]
> Polk Street
>
> Dear Frances,
> I have just acquired the most heart-rending symphony you ever heard. You must come to my mean hovel Saturday night to hear it, for I have to share it with you. In addition, there are two things I want to read to you, and a new picture I want you to see. Don't refuse, for I must see you, and I have laid in a store of Roquefort cheese as a special inducement. Yesterday and today I have been working spasmodically, and then drowning myself in music. I saw two girls on the streets this morning who reminded me of you.
> I'm going out to Charley's tonight, but I'll try to call you sometime tomorrow. Meanwhile, don't despair, for I'm trying not to.
> Love from Everett (125)

Frances must have had her hands full with this young artist whose passionate intensity could infuse even Roquefort cheese with romantic possibility. Though every lover will stand on the threshold of the Not-I, only a few press on into the misty hinterland of the other, what Roland Barthes calls the "Unknowable": "I am often struck by the obvious fact that the other is impenetrable, intractable, not to be found; I cannot open up the other, trace back the other's origins, solve the riddle. Where does the other come from? Who is the other? I wear myself out, I shall never know."[1]

---

1. *A Lover's Discourse*, p. 134.

Frances must have been astonished to stare into the eyes of eager Everett Ruess, only to discover an abyss far wider and deeper than the Grand Canyon. The romance dissolved quickly.

To scan the field of Ruess's carnal desire is to glean something of his desire for the wild—the two coeval come. Whereas carnal desire streams from the lover into the corporeal impoundment of the human beloved, desire for the wild expresses itself geographically, dispersed across and through entire swaths of Earth, charging the extensive space with potency. Such desire may be characterized by migrating nodes of intensity, now focused on a mountain, now on a river, a juniper, a tanager, a cougar, the sky itself. Anthropologists tell us that desire of this magnitude can only be turned to good account on the level of community—through its sense of place. Properly channeled, this rousing desire defines the familiar territories, charging them with meaning. Homesickness issues forth when this bond is ruptured. Though born into a culture lacking deep sensitivity to place, Ruess himself was attuned to its capacious circulations of desire. To wander slakes this lust.

For a time, around the winter solstice of 1933, while camped in his San Francisco "hovel" and making forays into the artistic community, he discovered the vast land-desire now localized in the woman Frances. It was a transference, a human embodiment of the *genius loci*: her presence, her being, became a frontier, a translator of desire, with the wild on one side, the human community on the other. This is the demand each lover, caught in the passionate flow, makes on the beloved: the demand for intimacy. But there is always the counterflow, what the dark Heraclitus called *enantiodromia*: "The way up and the way down are one in the same" (Fragment 60). Every relationship is analogous to lightning—stroke and counterstroke, establishing the circuit of desire. Tone depends upon intensity, the current. At times, when energy remains ungathered, desire in the lover is analogous to vague atmospheric static dispersed unnoticed across a region, while at other times it musters itself into the focused surges of lightning that shatter granite. Frances saw those dark thunderheads billowing up, and ran for shelter. The erotic torrent Ruess unleashed in her direction could not be impounded in the spa of an individual romance: he needed the community's extensive reservoirs—art and religion.

Nevertheless, how he speaks to Frances about himself, about their relationship, also speaks of his relationship to the wild, the whereof none can speak. Such speaking floods in contradiction. The beloved, in any given flow of desire, appears at times as a waterfall, at times as a rapid, but sometimes too as an unseen snag just below the surface, one of the many objects altering—indeed authoring—this uncanny hydrology. Writing from Chilchinbetoh, Arizona, on May 5, 1934, Everett Ruess released this freshet of words to Frances:

> To one aware of the strangeness of life, my life in the cities was as strange as it is here. In many ways, toward the last, it was a fulfillment. I had many gloriously beautiful experiences, as well as the wild and intense adventures which seem to come without my searching. I do not know if I shall ever return to the cities again, but I cannot complain that I found them empty of beauty.
>
> I was sorry, though, that our intimacy, like many things that are and will be, had to die with a dying fall. I do not greatly mind endings, for my life is made up of them, but sometimes they come too soon or too late, and sometimes they leave a feeling of regret as of an old mistake or an indirect futility. I like to be able to be perfectly open and sincere, and yet it is impossible to be sincere to all of one's self at once, so for the deepest understanding one must seek those with whom one can be most truly one's self. And never be blind to the ineffable drollery of it all.
>
> So here too I have been leading a life of strange contrasts, violent indeed when considered separately, yet flowing naturally enough into one another. There has been deep peace, vast calm and fury, strange comradeships and intimacies, and many times my life and all my possessions have tottered on the far side of the balance, but as yet, from each such encounter I have in the end come away, unharmed, and even toughened.
>
> But much as I love people, the most important thing to me is still the nearly unbearable beauty of what I see. I won't wish that you could see it, for you might not find it easy to bear either, but yet I do sincerely wish for you a little at least of the impossible. (145)

These are the words of a pilgrim, one who has already crossed the frontier and visited strange, indescribable territories, but Ruess is now homeward bound, partially transformed, and for a moment standing once again on a well-worn trail, the same path he had used on his journey outward. Tottering at last toward home, he is hesitating, unsure anymore that he even has a home, wavering between old and new grounds. He is a liminar, which literally means one who has crossed the threshold (L., *limen*, "threshold"). Every pilgrim is a potential emigrant. If the strange territories are more compelling, more enrapturing than the provenance, then an abandonment ensues. Everett Ruess would commit just such an abandonment six months later.

When he speaks in this letter to Frances of "unbearable beauty," what might he mean? When the mythologizers of his life inscribe his being within the signifier of "vagabond for beauty," what might they mean? What is meant by anybody's use of the word "beauty"? We say a particular landscape is "beautiful," and we say the beloved is "beautiful," but do we mean the same thing? Ralph Waldo Emerson, linking his use of the word *beauty* with the ancient Greek *Kosmos*, meaning "order, harmony," asserts: "The world thus exists to the soul to satisfy the desire of beauty." For Emerson, beauty as such is an "ultimate end" (Emerson, *Selected Writings* 14). When he peppers his discussion with such words as "delight," "pleasure," "order," and "reproductive," he is not attempting originality, but synthesis. Stendahl's suggestion that beauty is a "promise of happiness" provides a bridge from Emerson to Aristotle, who writes: "For, in a word, everything we choose we choose for the sake of something else—except happiness, which is an end" (Aristotle, *Selected Writings* 531). Beauty and happiness thus emerge from the ancient Greek philosopher as synonyms. We are able to know happiness as we are able to know beauty: by the pleasure of our perception. Whereas pleasure is the existential mark of happiness/beauty, manifesting itself in particular emotion, desire is always abstract, nonlocalized. Pleasure and desire, however, are inseparable; they cannot be cleaved: *pleasure is impounded desire*.

Pleasures differ in kind, Aristotle explains, with each kind "bound up with the activity it completes." Desire, on the other hand, is unimpeded, unchanneled flow; it knows no bounds, including words. Desire is wild. Pleasure, in the most concrete sense, is the beloved, that is, an impoundment: useful, knowable, indivisible from its object, subject of love poems, always at risk, because pleasure results from dams across the current. Desire, on the other hand, is the abstract flow, analogous to the hydrologic cycle, which is the "circuit of water movement from the atmosphere to the earth and return to the atmosphere through various stages or processes" (*Resource Conservation Glossary* 77). Unimpounded desire can never be "beautiful"; it is always and only unfathomable; whereas desire, in Aristotle's understanding, is "always separated both in time and in nature, pleasures are close to the activities, and so hard to distinguish from them that it admits of dispute whether the activity is not the same as the pleasure." In the end, there is only the pointing suggested in the opening chapter of the *Tao Te Ching*:

> The nameless wild is the origin of heaven and earth;
> Naming is the mother of the ten thousand things.
> Whenever there is no pleasure-or-pain, one beholds
>     the mystery;
> Whenever there is pleasure-or-pain, one beholds
>     the manifestation.
> Yet mystery and manifestation are the same, differ only
>     in name:
> Darkness within darkness, threshold of all understanding.

We take *pleasure* in the word *desire*, in the reckless adventure of defining it.

Not pleasure but its always attendant contrary—pain—is the mark of desire on Everett Ruess. He writes to Frances, his former beloved, of "unbearable beauty," indicating dangerous pressure of impounded desire. The river of Heraclitus is about to burst forth in turbulent draw: everything flows, nothing remains. The human beloved is insufficient catchment. Interestingly enough, the most sensual language Ruess ever used to express desire was not focused on a woman, but on a section of California coast. In one of his compositions, he writes:

> Then there will be no music but the sound of rushing water that breaks on pointed rocks far below, and the sighing of the wind in the pinyons—a warm wind that gently caresses my cheeks, ruffles my hair tenderly, and wanders downwards. Alone I will follow the dark trail, black void on one side and unattainable heights on the other,

darkness before and behind me, darkness that pulses and flows and is felt. Then suddenly an unreal breath of wind coming from infinite depths will bring to my ears again the strange, dimly-remembered sound of the rushing water. When that sound dies, all dies. (Rusho 21)

Even his own ego, that impoundment of subjectivity, is fragmented under such pressure. Ruess laments his inability to be "sincere to all of one's self at once," the many selves. The flow of desire that was the ego now unravels into a braided stream, having abandoned the need for a main channel, indicating proximity to the ocean. Freud, in *Civilization and Its Discontents*, described this "oceanic feeling" as "a sensation of 'eternity,' a feeling as of something limitless, unbounded . . . " (11). Others simply call it the mystical, which is "the apprehension of one thing doing everything" (Watts, *Tao* 94).

When Ruess tells Frances "many times my life and all my possessions have tottered on the far side of balance," he is not boasting, but speaking literally and figuratively. More than once, he had seen his pack animals lose their footing and tumble from a steep trail; more than once, he himself had taken spills. On a figurative level, he is referring to the state of his soul, the fragment of ambiguous space that is his self. The self is an improbable bundle of perceptions, life's constant performance through space and time. Consciousness, that shining limited clarity, is a glade in the wild forest, and the ego loves the glade, declares this to be the only ground of the self. The ego is uninterested in, or incapable of, venturing into the dark forest for fear of becoming subsumed by the dark wood, so it hacks away at the margins and attempts to widen the glade. To drop the axe and venture into the wooly wild is to unself the self—"to quit myself like a man," says Bunyan's Christian; to plunge into Emily Dickinson's "Wild Nights—Wild Nights!":

> Were I with thee
> Wild Nights should be
> Our luxury!
>
> Futile—the Winds—
> To a Heart in port—

Done with the Compass—
Done with the Chart!

More prosaically, we might adopt the language of psychology to say
that Ruess's letters show the signs of an incipient psychosis; or to
be less pathological, we may borrow the terms of anthropology and
say that Ruess seems to be experiencing a state of "liminality," a
phase of decisive experiential change in which "previous orderings
of thought and behavior are subject to revision and criticism,
when hitherto unprecedented modes of ordering relations between
ideas and people become possible and desirable" (Victor and Edith
Turner 2). Even so, to attribute "decisiveness" to Everett Ruess
would be inappropriate; such decisiveness is characteristic of a will
to power, tyrannical to some degree, capable of organizing the unfamiliar—that willfulness found in artists like Edward Weston.
Ruess, on the other hand, despite the bravado of his letters, is—to
use again his own word—"tottering." He becomes decisive only in
his end, in his disappearance. And even in this we cannot be sure.

A curious manifestation of his tottering reveals itself in a series
of letters wherein he relates a peculiar transposing of proper
names—between himself and his burro. For two months, in 1931,
he was signing his letters "Lan Rameau," a self-fashioned sobriquet
he hoped would be swanky enough for currency in the art world.
"Please respect my brush name," he begs of his family. "It is hard to
lead a dual existence" (Rusho 29). The letter goes on, in apparent
earnestness: "The first name begins with 'L,' not 'S.' How do you
say it in French? Nomme de broushe, or what? I would like to
know. If you use my new name in addressing letters it will save
confusion. It's not the perfect cognomen but I intend to stick by
it." The name "Everett Ruess," having been displaced but not dis-
lodged altogether, migrated over to the burro: "I call him Everett,
to remind me of the kind of person I used to be." The new appella-
tion seems to have caused him some problems, as later he writes,
still devoid of irony: "I have changed my name again, to Evert
Rulan. Those who knew me formerly thought my name was freak-
ish and an affectation of Frenchiness. *It is not easy to choose a name*,
but Evert Rulan can be spelled, pronounced, remembered and is
moderately distinctive" (37). He maintained himself as "Evert

Rulan" until the end of 1931, when, without fanfare, he reverted to Everett Ruess, the first and last name he would ever have. The need to change one's name suggests a rite of passage practiced in many cultures, a rite that signposts an important psychological juncture in the tribal individual's life. Ruess had clearly arrived at an important juncture, but he lacked the guidance, the cultural framework, that provides the context for successful passage.[2] He was on his own.

The bestowing of a name is a cultural act, establishing the individual's place in the community. The name remains community property, not the individual's. Conferred upon the individual at birth, it is indicative of the community's authority. The individual, over the course of the life, may choose to change names, but this does not guarantee the change; ultimately, the community must recognize the switch, *employ the new name itself*, and thus validate it through usage—otherwise, it is null and void. The individual who seeks to change identity, the immigrant or the fugitive, is always at risk with an alias: the old name, the "true" identity, can at any time come back to haunt. Should the community so decide, the new is dissolved by the old. The individual who seeks to escape the name, the identity, can do so only by becoming "no one," NEMO. Herein lies the individual's genuine freedom. The community, however, remains fully capable of imagining the one who chooses to become "no one"; indeed, the community can imagine a one-never-known, a one-who-escaped utterly into the wild—and in these imaginings, in fashioning these myths and legends around such a one, *the community brings that one back*. The *terra incognita* so called is not the true wild because it can be named and thereby known. The wild is always just out of reach: It withdraws before this sentence.

Everett Ruess, as he can be known from letters preserved and published, stands on the frontier that desire must cross before it can be impounded. According to Anne Carson, letters are erotic products. "Letters construct the space of desire and kindle in it these contradictory emotions that keep the lover alert to his own impasses. . . . From within letters, Eros acts" (92). The individual

---

2. See Arnold van Gennep, *The Rites of Passage*.

human, *homo faber*, sometimes channels surplus desire into a letter, which is but one of the ten thousand containments.

Art is another. One can glean this by surveying what artists themselves—especially romantic ones—have had to say about art. Emerson writes: "The poet, the painter, the sculptor, the musician, the architect, seek to concentrate this radiance of the world on one point, and each in his several work to satisfy the love of beauty which stimulates him to produce. Thus is Art a nature passed through the alembic of man. Thus in art does Nature work through the will of a man filled with the beauty of her first works" (Emerson, *Selected Writings* 14). This same plasticity of imagination, in all its playfulness, is the experience of childhood.[3] Recall this for yourself. What separates the adult from the child is the former's capacity for dead seriousness. Adults have their burdens, envy those who travel light.

Missing from Ruess's letter to Frances is any mention of art, any mention of his artistic ambitions—which is unusual for him. With characteristic bluster, he asserts in a 1931 letter to his brother: "It is my intention to accomplish something very definite in Art" (Rusho 43). More than once in his letters is the assurance, "I'm confident I can make something of my work," though he immediately adds, "the problem is how to keep alive until I begin to succeed in a larger measure" (66, 67). To his artist mother, he discourses on technique: "The other day I had perhaps the best art lesson I ever had; a lesson in simplicity from Maynard Dixon. That time I really did learn something, I think, and I have been trying to apply what I learned. The main thing Maynard did was to make me see what is meaningless in a picture, and have the strength to eliminate it; and see what was significant, and how to stress it" (118). The references in his letters to art, expressed in terms of career and technique, are much more numerous during the first years of his wanderings; toward the end of his correspondence, the dilettantish imaginings are displaced by impassioned declarations about "beauty" and the inability of anyone to express it. "But he who has looked long on naked beauty may never return to the world, and though he should try, he will find its occupation empty and vain,

---

3. See Edith Cobb, *The Ecology of Imagination in Childhood.*

and human intercourse purposeless and futile" (148). With its barely suppressed eroticism, this statement could easily be dismissed as romantic swaggering or, less generously, may be tucked safely into the Freudian's oedipal bed. Given Ruess's eventual disappearance, it is more playful, more intriguing, to regard his words as a pilgrim's expression of liminality.

To pass over the limen, the margin, the periphery of the known, is to disappear into the open, the anonymous, the uncarved block. The liminal state, according to the anthropologists Turner, "has frequently been likened to death; to being in the womb; to invisibility, darkness, bisexuality, and the wilderness" (Victor and Edith Turner 249). On one level, this is Dante's Inferno—but Ruess lacks his Virgil. "I have gone too far alone" (Rusho 160), he acknowledges in the end. In abandoning faith in "human intercourse," he also abandons faith in a media-based art, in any attempt he might make as an individual to conduct, through word or sketch, the desire that overwhelms him. Instead he chooses to abandon *himself* to desire through the art of *performance*. He unselfs himself; relinquishes Name, Word, and Body; disappears into the wild; and becomes "NEMO."

Walking those thousands of miles, much of it off trail, was his performance, the pounding of human foot on earth, leaving its trace, its tread, its reverberation on and in the sensible world. The complex, utterly improbable movement of the human body—the breath, the heartbeat, the turn, the dance, the *walk*—constitutes human passage across the world. All pilgrims, in their walking, in their moving bodies, fundamentally express the wild. If the pilgrim happens also to be an artist, the question becomes: How embody this wildness, convey this perception to others? If the pilgrim is a writer: How make words wild? It is not enough to write *about* the wild. Most writing about nature—and nearly all writing about wilderness—is quite tame, informing a reader about conventions, ideologies, and habits rather than unleashing the flood that overwhelms as it erases. Were it only for his writing, Everett Ruess would be of little interest to most readers today. His prose is at times pretentious, at times lackluster, often imitative, always adolescent—but it maintains an air of sweetness. If the *puer aeternus* in one's own self is close to the surface—as it seems to be in the band of mythologizers who keep Ruess's memory alive—one can forgive him, perhaps even (secretly) envy him, despite the fact that his prose is less than superb.

Yet, in his walking, as one who knew and sought the wild, Ruess was a preeminent performance artist. He took his art to the very threshold of possibility, to the verge of empty space, to *nowhere*—and then, in his greatest, never-to-be-repeated performance, unwitnessed—he dropped art altogether, unharnessed his burden, and stepped across the margin, never to return. When the self goes wild, it is never seen again. "The rain washed away my tracks. The saddle is well cached. The ghosts of the cliff dwellers will guard it. I do not think I will return for it, however" (83). Many times Ruess promised to disappear, and his letters provide ample testimony: "In the meantime, my burro and I, and a little dog, if I can find one, are going on and on, until, sooner or later, we reach the end of the horizon" (40). (Ruess eventually did find a little dog that joined him in his wanderings; however, the canine beat Everett to the punch—by disappearing first!) "I must pack my short life full of interesting events and creative activity. Philosophy and aesthetic contemplation are not enough. I intend to do everything possible to broaden my experiences and allow myself to reach the fullest development. Then, and before physical deterioration obtrudes, I shall go on some last wilderness trip, to a place I have known and loved. I shall not return" (44). "I'll never stop wandering. And when the time comes to die, I'll find the wildest, loneliest, most desolate spot there is" (78). And in the last letter anyone was to receive from him, he writes: "As to when I shall visit civilization, it will not be soon, I think. I have not tired of the wilderness; rather I enjoy its beauty and the vagrant life I lead, more keenly all the time. . . . Even from your scant description, I know that I could not bear the routine and humdrum of the life that you are forced to lead. I don't think I could ever settle down. I have known too much of the depths of life already and would prefer anything to anticlimax" (178–79). All of these words would only add up to so much cant were it not for one thing: The promise was made good. Everett Ruess disappeared—and therein lies the art.

To the degree that each of us fears disappearance, fears becoming a missing person or becoming unknown, fears death, we collectively direct desire against this possibility by participating in community projects: mythology, folklore, legend, gossip. We build monuments to the unknown soldier and turn him into an Everyman, feel a greater pull in the stomach when we pass the potter's field than the ordinary graveyard with its shining tombstone names, tell stories about the missing, about the departed, and, if need be, tailor for them rapacious ghosts—and in our saying "they haunt such and such a place," *we keep them here.*

It is toward this erogenous zone of our collective psyche that Everett Ruess pitched his performance, his art, his disappearance; through this effort, he induced a rupture, opened a channel of desire that threatened to surge and overwhelm us all. As a group, as a community, as a society, despite whatever we may say to the contrary, we do not tolerate a becoming unknown, whether involuntary or willful. Human existence, we like to believe, has a teleology in the opposite direction. Thus, if you disappear, your photo will turn up in police files, on television screens, on milk cartons. It is illegal to kill yourself. Ruess's act—including his last word, "NEMO"—challenges the herd's injunction that one may never leave the herd. When it was recognized that Ruess had in fact disappeared, the president of Utah's Associated Civic Clubs mobilized his fellow members to fund a search for the missing boy. The rallying cry for the posse was: "No one gets lost in southern Utah!" (192). Nemo. Even boosterism is cast toward maintaining the sanctity of individual identity—*by keeping track.* No one escapes in the manner of the flagrant Everett Ruess.

In his "NEMO" Ruess issued the human community a threat: "I *can* disappear." Society has responded to this quintessential betrayal by turning him into a legend. Thus, we will always harbor the suspicion that *this* is really what he was seeking all along: He wasn't the free radical he would have us believe, but rather an artist, playing a well-established role within the community, thus incapable of renouncing his communicative responsibility. The artists Ruess had befriended knew this, and their words convey the community's anxiety over his disappearance. Maynard Dixon, upon learning of Ruess's apparent fate, wrote to Stella and Christopher Ruess: "That is certainly distressing news. But wanderers like Everett have disappearing habits—and he may yet show up. We wish you luck in your search" (182). Similarly, Hamlin Garland, who knew much about main-traveled roads, wrote: "Your son was a most unusual spirit. I have never known a youth of like endowment and predilection. He is a most interesting character. If he should ever come out of hiding he will bring a noble book in his knapsack!" (207). And then Edward Weston, apparently affirming the performative nature of Ruess's art, declared: "The way of his going, I feel, is the way I would like to depart—close to the soil. But he was so young" (198). If nothing else, Ruess's performance has had the effect of transmogrifying into an artist anybody who continues to fashion his legend.

Everett Ruess, as I have been telling his story, seems a strange figure to use as representative of what I will have to say about four American writers who take as their subject "the wild." He is no writer in the traditional sense—as Henry David Thoreau, John Muir, Clarence King, and Mary Hunter Austin are received as writers. Everett Ruess, if we deem him an artist, is a performance artist. Indeed, all writers of the wild are performance artists, to the extent that in their lives and bodies they had experiences they identified as "wild"—in the same way that all humans have such experiences, even if they never leave their houses. To borrow a phrase from John Muir, "Going out is really going in." The wild is as much inside as outside.

Everett Ruess was a pilgrim to the wild, of the most extreme order—because he did not return. Of what use, then, is language or art? Language and art are born of the wild, but they are not the wild; they are conventions, collectively impounded desire, but in their intensity they still flow—and this, as so many philosophers have concluded, is what we call beauty, happiness, pleasure, and, just as often, pain. Ruess is the zero-degree writer. His "NEMO" is the last word before the wild. No words are possible beyond this point. He has piled the outermost cairn, and there is no sign of a trail past here. It is the *ne plus ultra* that all pilgrims must pass, and in passing they are thus un-formed; should they manage to return, they have been trans-formed, and they may feel compelled to write of their pilgrim experience.

If it is true that "life is a journey," then each of us is a pilgrim and every writer is a travel writer. Too often so-called nature writers confine their subjects to limited territories, mere glades of description; in their more adventurous moments, they tend to seize upon a moral. Emerson demonstrates this tendency when he claims that "every natural process is a moral sentence," deferring mention that the world generates an infinite number of moralities to suit an infinite number of interpreters. In the course of a more wanton roving, a writer may encounter what seems to be an immovable truth—proclaims "This is it!" and stops going further. Many end their journeys by crashing into stone walls of reification—words such as "nature" or "wilderness." Such writers are ecomoralists, concerned with cultural construction, not clarity of perception; party to ideology, not impact. They issue jeremiads.

In the meditations that follow, I muse on four writers who in constituting a significant cluster in the tradition of American nature writing simultaneously ambulate far beyond its pale. Taking the wild as their subject, they are engaged—to varying degrees of self-consciousness—in the writer's struggle with the impossible: to write that which cannot be written; to write about themselves in relation to that which cannot be written; and to write about themselves in relation to their communities.

Once again, Everett Ruess is the rule-proving exception. In his rejection of media-based art, including writing, he declines the challenge that Thoreau, Muir, King, and Austin all accept. In so declining, he becomes a traitor—to writing. He betrays language itself—and the whole human community—by walking away. He plunged into a freedom that contemporary wilderness aficionados only dream about. But the freedom comes at the highest price—everything, including the name. No one is *most free*. Nemo. There is a pathos in the 1931 letter Ruess signed with his "nomme de broushe" Lan: "Somehow I don't feel like writing now, or even talking. Both actions seem superfluous. If you were here, you might understand, but too much is incommunicable. If I were there—but that is unthinkable. You cannot understand what aeons and spaces are between us" (39). In the works (and sometimes the lives) of the four writers I will discuss, I hope to show that they, like Ruess, are aware that "too much is incommunicable." Nevertheless, *they strive to communicate*, in widely divergent ways, and they often fail or come up short. They too grapple with issues of freedom, but none of them free themselves to the degree that the impossible Everett Ruess freed himself.

The question every writer confronts, consciously or not, is: How can I succeed when the task, from the beginning, is impossible? As I cast my own net into the waters of desire, attempting now myself to write about what others have written about that which cannot be written, I sense the same aeons and spaces between myself and my subject, myself and my audience. There is nothing wild about a book. One writes it only to escape from having to write it. Talk about the impossible. To borrow Ruess's words one more time, among the last he ever offered to his former lover: "I do sincerely wish for you a little at least of the impossible."

# TWO

# Henry David Thoreau
# Sauntering along the Edge

> *"First you go over to the other side to find out it exists,*
> *then you come back to this side to act."*
> —Ancient Zen Master

### Practicing Faithfully

When readers of *The Atlantic Monthly* opened the magazine in June of 1862 they found themselves confronted with a declamation. Bearing the unlikely title of "Walking," it began: "I wish to speak a word for Nature, for absolute freedom and wildness, as contrasted with a freedom and culture merely civil,—to regard man as an inhabitant, or a part and parcel of Nature, rather than a member of society" (657). The audience (most of it) was unaware they were listening to a ghost. Though the speaker of these words, Henry David Thoreau, had passed away the previous month, he was to prove a persistent revenant, brazen past the end. "I wish to make an extreme statement, if so I may make an emphatic one, for there are enough champions of civilization: the minister, the school-committee, and every one of you will take care of that."

Thoreau's prose remains unsettling, brimming with what his friend and neighbor Ralph Waldo Emerson termed "a certain petulance." Thoreau himself once cautioned a correspondent: "I trust that you realize what an exaggerator I am,—that I lay myself out to exaggerate whenever I have the opportunity,—pile Pelion upon Ossa, to reach heaven so" (*Corr* 304). The word *exaggerate*, rising into English from Latin, literally means "to pile up." As a writer, Thoreau sometimes does pile it *on*, but more often *up*—making a mountain out of what most would say is ordinary life. This pilgrim's path to the wild leads through the everyday details, mounting the quotidian, to arrive at last right where he and his reader began. "I do not know that knowledge amounts to anything more definite than a novel and grand surprise, or a sudden revelation of

the insufficiency of all that we had called knowledge before; an in-
definite sense of the grandeur and glory of the universe" (J:ii 168).
If Thoreau's writing offers any lesson it would be, as he expressed it
himself in another letter, "Do what you love" (*Corr* 216).

Thoreau loved to walk and he loved to write—for him, the two
loves were inseparable. Nowhere in his work is this more evident
than in "Walking," wherein he informs his reader that he prefers
the word *saunter* to describe the practice of his love:

> I have met with but one or two persons in the course of my life who
> understood the art of Walking, that is, of taking walks,—who had a
> genius, so to speak, for *sauntering*: which word is beautifully derived
> "from idle people who roved about the country, in the Middle Ages,
> and asked charity, under pretence of going *a la Sainte Terre*," to the
> Holy Land, till the children exclaimed, "There goes a *Sainte-Terrer*,"
> a Saunterer,—a Holy Lander. (657)

Although Thoreau's etymology here can be traced only to his
imagination, it underscores the linkage between walking and pilgrimage. Each of his walks—whether in Concord or further
afield—is a pilgrimage. In his characteristic style of exaggeration,
he concludes the paragraph: "For every walk is a sort of crusade,
preached by some Peter the Hermit in us, to go forth and recon-
quer this Holy Land from the hands of the Infidels." A crusade is
pilgrimage with a vengeance.

If we take Thoreau literally, we risk missing his point: The
walker is a pilgrim, a stranger in a strange land, unfettered by the
conventions of everyday life. The essay "Walking" is a diligent inquiry into the erotics of writing—not a credo, but an account of
one writer's practice, Thoreau's great disquisition on the imagination. Sauntering, he tells us, is a frame of mind. "Some, however,
would derive the word from *sans terre*, without land or a home,
which, therefore, in the good sense, will mean having no particular
home, but equally at home everywhere. For this is the secret of
successful sauntering" (657). The Buddhists, Gary Snyder tells us,
use the word *homeless* to designate a monk or priest. "It refers to a
person who has supposedly left the householder's life and the
temptations and obligations of the secular world behind" (103).
This is the same "good sense" of the word saunter—*sans terre*—
that Thoreau intends.

Translations of the rich philosophical literature of Asia were just beginning to appear in European languages in the 1830s and 1840s, and Thoreau was among the first American readers to discover them. In 1849, having already consumed several English and French translations of "Hindu" texts, he writes to Harrison Blake: "Depend upon it that rude and careless as I am, I would fain practise the *yoga* faithfully" (*Corr* 251). He practiced the "yoga"—that is, "skill in action"—by walking, and he practiced writing by composing in his *Journal*.

> I must walk more with free senses. It is as bad to *study* stars and clouds as flowers and stones. I must let my senses wander as my thoughts, my eyes see without looking. Carlyle said that how to observe was to look, but I say that it is rather to see, and the more you look the less you will observe. I have the habit of attention to such excess that my senses get no rest, but suffer from a constant strain. Be not preoccupied with looking. Go not to the object; let it come to you. When I have found myself looking down and confining my gaze to the flowers, I have thought it might be well to get into the habit of observing the clouds as a corrective, but no! that study would be just as bad. What I need is not to look at all, but a true sauntering of the eye. (J:iv 351)

A "true sauntering of the eye" is Thoreau's way of describing a form of perception free of any irritable reaching of ego-mind after objects and facts, a way of "seeing" that overcomes the mind–body dichotomy. The goal of Thoreau's practice is to saunter in mind as well as in body–the two are one. He called this "pure mind."[1]

The *Journal* entry for December 25, 1851, provides a detailed contrast between the "vulgar" and "pure" mind:

---

1. Of Thoreau's many critics, Sharon Cameron comes closest to identifying the *practice* that informs the entire *Journal*: "The consequence of the doubleness and of the displacement of human perspective as I have been describing them are (1) a form of analogy which seems unfamiliar to us, for through it the mind becomes the receptacle for material that is alien to it; (2) an entire book predicated on such analogies in which the terms of the ordinary hierarchy that subordinates nature to human nature (and the ordinary way of bridging the difference between the two, by likening nature to the mind) are suspended and transposed" (149). I would take her observations here one step further: (1) the mind, in Thoreau's practice, is not a "receptacle" but *is* nature; and (2) there is no "bridging" between nature and human nature: if anything, the two are one; let us say it is the river that Cameron imagines needs a bridge.

It would be a truer discipline for the writer to take the least film of thought that floats in the twilight sky of his mind for his theme, about which he has scarcely one idea (that would be teaching his ideas how to shoot), faintest intimations, shadowiest subjects, make a lecture on this, by assiduity and attention get perchance two views of the same, increase a little the stock of knowledge, clear a new field instead of manuring the old; instead of making a lecture out of such obvious truths, hackneyed to the minds of all thinkers. We seek too soon to ally the perceptions of the mind to the experience of the hand, to prove our gossamer truths practical, to show their connection with our every-day life (better show their distance from our every-day life), to relate them to the cider-mill and the banking institution. Ah, give me pure mind, pure thought! Let me not be in haste to detect the *universal law*; let me see more clearly a particular instance of it! Much finer themes I aspire to, which will yield no satisfaction to the vulgar mind, not one sentence for them. (J:iii 156–57)

This passage rings with the familiar Thoreauvian self-reliance, much misunderstood as misty transcendentalism or mere orneriness, but in the context of his practice, of his *discipline*, it is evident that he identifies the "vulgar mind" as a cluttered mind, as perception clouded by "the common sense." When Thoreau calls himself a "Transcendentalist," he means that he is one who disciplines his perception to transcend the common sense. "This, our respectable daily life," he writes to Blake, "in which the man of common sense, the Englishman of the world, stands so squarely, and on which our institutions are founded, is in fact the veriest illusion, and will vanish like the baseless fabric of a vision" (*Corr* 215).

Emerson writes of Thoreau that he was a "born protestant. . . . If he slighted and defied the opinions of others, it was only that he was more intent to reconcile his practice with his own belief" (*Selected Writings* 896). Thus, in "Walking," when Thoreau declares, "In my walks I would fain return to my senses" ("Walking" 659), we should read it with a stress on the pronoun *my*, not in any egomaniacal sense but as "the doors of perception cleansed," as pure mind.

This pilgrim seeks clarity of mind, clarity in the same *un*-common sense that the poet George Oppen seeks it:

*Clarity*

In the sense of *transparence*,
I don't mean that much can be explained.

Clarity in the sense of silence.
(*Collected Poems* 162)

Clarity in silence. "This stillness," Thoreau writes in 1852, "is more impressive than any sound. The moon [—] the stars—the trees—the snow—the sand where bare—a monumental stillness—whose void must be supplanted by thought—it extracts thought from the beholder, as the void under a cupping glass raises a swelling. How much a silent mankind might suggest!" (J:iii 340–41). When Daniel Ricketson, the most persistent of Thoreau's correspondents, rebukes him for a recent lapse in correspondence, the author of *Walden* counters: "Why will you waste so many regards on me, and not know what to think of my silence? Infer from it what you might from the silence of a dense pine wood. It is its natural condition, except when the winds blow, and the jays scream, & the chickadee winds up his clock. My silence is just as inhuman as that, and no more" (*Corr* 599). Silence is the whereof we cannot speak. Silence is wild.

A riddle, too, is wild, especially if it has no "answer" amenable to words. Zen Buddhists call such a riddle a *koan*, a fundamental point, first principle, or truth that is experienced directly. One of the most famous Thoreau passages is a "riddle" sifted out from *Walden*: "I long ago lost a hound, a bay horse and a turtle-dove, and am still on their trail. Many are the travellers I have spoken concerning them, describing their tracks, and what calls they answered to. I have met one or two who have heard the hound, and the tramp of the horse, and even seen the dove disappear behind a cloud; and they seemed as anxious to recover them as if they had lost them themselves." Readers are wont to ask: "To what is he referring? What does a hound, a bay horse, and a turtle-dove symbolize?"

This passage has been a persistent source of reader anxiety ever since *Walden*'s first publication. A year or two after the book came out, the story goes, Thoreau encountered a man in Plymouth, Massachusetts, who asked him what he meant by the passage. The author is alleged to have responded: "Well, Sir, I suppose we have all our losses." "That's a pretty way to answer a fellow," the man replied (*Variorum Walden* 270). The obvious rancor in this man's words can be attributed to having been denied a common-sense response to a common-sense question. Thoreau simply is not interested in the common sense as such—save to clear it from his own perception. As he explains in a letter to the businessman Benjamin Wiley:

> How shall we account for our pursuits if they are original? We get the language which to describe our various lives out of a common mint. If others have their losses, which they are busy repairing, so have I *mine*, & their hound & horse may *perhaps* be the symbols of some of them. But also I have lost, or am in danger of losing, a far finer & more ethereal treasure, which commonly no loss of which they are conscious will symbolize—this I answer hastily & with some hesitation, according as I now understand my words. (*Corr* 478)

Thoreau treads his own path; even language is insufficient to give account of it, for language itself is part of the common sense. Thus, he "plays" with words (using rhetorical "tricks" as Emerson would phrase it), well aware of their inadequacy. As a writer, he relentlessly fronts the linguistic edge. At one time, he intended as an epigraph for *Walden* the couplet: "Where I have been / There none was seen" (qtd. in Golemba 108). This is one way of expressing "pure mind."

Pure mind emerges when the vulgar mind, the common sense, is silenced; pure mind is not a matter of knowledge, of "learning" in the traditional sense, but a rigorous *un*-learning. "I have nothing to learn," he writes to Blake in 1853, "but something to practise" (*Corr* 297). In the *Journal*, he writes: "How much forbearance, aye, sacrifice and loss, goes to every accomplishment! I am thinking by what long discipline and at what cost a man learns to speak simply at last" (J:iii 134).

## An Awful Ferity

The pilgrim seeks estrangement from the familiar. "Two or three hours' walking will carry me to as strange a country as I expect ever to see" ("Walking" 660). Estrangement (from the Latin *extraneus*, literally "not belonging to a community or place") is predicated upon crossing boundaries, leaving the known for the unknown. It is a liminal phenomenon. Long before Frederick Jackson Turner, Thoreau recognized in the disappearance of the physical frontier a powerful symbolic potential. In his first book, he relates the discovery that the land north of Massachusetts (that is, New Hampshire, including the rugged White Mountains) is already well settled:

> But we found the frontiers were not this way any longer. This generation has come into the world fatally late for some enterprises. Go where we will on the *surface* of things, men have been there before us. We cannot now have the pleasure of erecting the *last* house; that was long ago set up in the suburbs of Astoria city, and our boundaries have literally been run to the South Sea, according to the old patents. . . . The frontiers are not east or west, north or south, but wherever a man *fronts* a fact, though that fact be his neighbor, there is an unsettled wilderness between him and Canada, between him and the setting sun, or, further still, between him and *it*. Let him build himself a log-house with the bark on where he is, *fronting* IT, and wage there an Old French war for seven or seventy years, with Indians and Rangers, or whatever else may come between him and the reality, and save his scalp if he can. ( *Week* 303–4)

The pilgrim, in crossing the frontier, fronts IT. IT? A third-person pronoun, writ large so it can't be missed—but what is its referent? We might say "Nature," or the "unconscious," or the "uncarved block," or some other name, but all are inadequate. "I will not allow mere names to make distinctions for me," he writes in "Walking" (670). This is the problem with naming, the problem with assigning terms; ultimately, it is the problem with language itself, haunting all of our intellectual pursuits, including science. "Whatever aid is to be derived from the use of a scientific term," Thoreau writes in the *Journal*, "we can never begin to see anything as it is so long as we remember the scientific term which always our ignorance has imposed on it. Natural objects and phenomena are in this sense forever wild and unnamed by us" (J:xiii 141). Language does not provide a means or vehicle for fronting IT.

Walking, a verb disguised as a noun, is Thoreau's method for fronting IT, fronting the wild. Unlike Everett Ruess, he does not *plunge into* IT, does not disappear, does not sacrifice his identity as a writer, but keeps his distance, keeps to the edges from which he sends dispatches back to the community.

> I find that it is an excellent walk for variety and novelty and wild-ness, to keep round the edge of the meadow. . . . a narrow, meander-ing walk, rich in unexpected views and objects. The line of rubbish which marks the higher tides—withered flags and reeds and twigs and cranberries—is to my eyes a very agreeable and significant line, which Nature traces along the edge of the meadows. (J:ii 153–54)

Keeping to the edge, keeping distance between him and IT, is es-sential—as it is in any erotic relationship. And Thoreau is, after all, well aware of the mechanisms of Eros. In 1842, he writes in the *Journal*:

> My friend is cold and reserved because his love for me is waxing and not waning. These are the early processes; the particles are just begin-ning to shoot in crystals. If the mountains came to me, I should no longer go to the mountains. So soon as that consummation takes place which I wish, it will be past. Shall I not have a friend in re-serve? Heaven is to come. I hope this is not *it*. (J:i 339, emphasis added)

When Thoreau speaks of "fronting IT," this is but another way of referring to desire itself; but desire ends in consummation, wherein IT, rather than fronted, is expropriated, embodied in the pleasure-or-pain of the moment, thus eliminating the distance. The word *desire* is derived from an ancient Indo-European verb that means "to shine." In Latin, this becomes *sidus*, "star or con-stellation." Meandering through various linguistic bayous, it comes to us in modern English as "consider," a word that literally means "to observe the stars carefully." The stars are a long way off, and so too the object of desire; thus, we have "longing." Once the dis-tance is eliminated, so too the desire.

> To-day you may write a chapter on the advantages of travelling, and to-morrow you may write another chapter on the advantages of not travelling. The horizon has one kind of beauty and attraction to him who has never explored the hills and mountains in it, and another, I fear a less ethereal and glorious one, to him who has. That blue

mountain in the horizon is certainly the most heavenly, the most elysian, which we have not climbed, on which we have not camped for a night. But only our horizon is moved further off, and if our whole life should prove thus a failure, the future which is to atone for all, where still there might be some success, will be more glorious still. (J:iii 106–7)

"Heard melodies are sweet," says Keats, "but those unheard are sweeter." Or as Thoreau once said to Emerson: "What you seek in vain for, half your life, one day you come full upon, all the family at dinner. You seek it like a dream, and as soon as you find it you become its prey" (Emerson, *Selected Writings* 906). This observation is perhaps derived from Thoreau's experience as a writer, the need he felt to establish a distance between himself and the object of his pen, akin to Wordsworth's "emotion recollected in tranquility." "I succeed best," Thoreau explains in the *Journal*, "when I *recur* to my experience not too late but within a day or two, when there is some distance, but enough of freshness" (J:iv 20). Distance is all, for lover and for writer.[2]

Thoreau's reports, his writings, are finally acts of love issued from the edge of civilization, which is also the edge of the wild. "My Journal should be the record of my love. I would write in it only of the things I love, my affection for any aspect of the world, what I love to think of" (J:ii 101). Regarding his love, he makes an even more emphatic point on January 30, 1852:

Do nothing merely out of good resolutions. Discipline yourself only to yield to love; suffer yourself to be attracted. It is vain to write on chosen themes. We must wait till they have kindled a flame in our minds. There must be the copulating and generating force of love behind every effort destined to be successful. The cold resolve gives birth to, begets, nothing. The theme that seeks me, not I it. The

---

2. In the same vein, a passage from the *Journal* (August 27, 1859): "All our life, i.e., the living part of it, is a persistent dreaming awake. The boy does not camp in his father's yard. That would not be adventurous enough, there are too many sights and sound to disturb the illusion; so he marches off twenty or thirty miles and there pitches his tent, where stranger inhabitants are tamely sleeping in their beds just like his father at home, and camps in *their* yard, perchance. But then he dreams uninterruptedly that he is anywhere but where he is" (J:xii 296–97).

poet's relation to his theme is the relation of lovers. It is no more to
be courted. Obey, report. (J:iii 253)

In "Walking," he asserts: "The wildness of the savage is but a faint
symbol of the awful ferity with which good men and lovers meet"
(669). Like all lovers, Thoreau lingers on the edge of himself; from
here he writes.

To bring ego consciousness to its very boundary is, in fact, to
run the risk of dissolution. We call this "living on the edge." Here,
the common sense fails: there is no civilization, there is no wild;
there is no you, there is no me; there is no mind, there is no body.
All is one. Edges—those sharp distinctions—are scats of limited
perception. When ecologists refer to an "edge," they mean the
transitional zone where one community blends into another; this
edge, or frontier, is characterized by special environmental conditions—often called the "edge effect"—derived from both communities, generating an intrinsic space unto itself. These edges between ecological communities are sometimes called "ecotones"
(*tone* is derived from the Greek *teinein*, "to stretch"). Boundaries
such as these—similar to those that define moments in time—
have no distinct demarcations; instead, they are zones of blending.

Thoreau realized that the edge, the limen, is not a simple two-
dimensional line, but a vast erotic space. "Eros," Anne Carson tells
us, "is an issue of boundaries," a phenomenon of the limen.

> He exists because certain boundaries do. In the interval between
> reach and grasp, between glance and counterglance, between "I love
> you" and "I love you too," the absent presence of desire comes alive.
> But the boundaries of time and glance and I love you are only after-
> shocks of the main, inevitable boundary that creates Eros: the bound-
> ary of flesh and self between you and me. And it is only, suddenly, at
> the moment when I would dissolve that boundary, I realize I never
> can. (Carson 30)

There is power inherent in space; all writers of the wild sense it
and attempt to express it through the written word. Thoreau's
*Journal* is filled with accounts of his perception of the sheer power
of space. On January 7, 1851, he writes: "I felt my spirits rise when
I had got off the road into the open fields, and the sky had a new
appearance. I stepped along more buoyantly. There was a warm

sunset over the wooded valleys, a yellowish tinge on the pines. Reddish dun-colored clouds like dusky flames stood over it. And then streaks of blue sky were seen here and there. The life, the joy, that is in blue sky after a storm! There is no account of the blue sky in history. Before I walked in the ruts of travel; now I adventured" (J:ii 138–39). Carson points out that the troubadours referred to courtly love as *L'amour d'loonh*, "love from a distance." Love is a liminal phenomenon; to find oneself *in* love is to perceive the erotic space that lies between lover and beloved, real and ideal, actual and imagined, is and ought. This perception is contingent upon triangulation:

> For, where eros is lack, its activation calls for three structural components—lover, beloved and that which comes between them. They are three points of transformation on a circuit of possible relationship, electrified by desire so that they touch not touching. Conjoined they are held apart. The third component plays a paradoxical role for it both connects and separates, marking that two are not one, irradiating the absence whose presence is demanded by eros. When the circuit-points connect, perception leaps. And something becomes visible, on the triangular path where volts are moving, that would not be visible without the three-part structure. The difference between what is and what could be is visible. The ideal is projected on a screen of the actual, in a kind of stereoscopy . . . two poles of response within the same desiring mind. Triangulation makes both present at once by a shift of distance, replacing erotic action with a ruse of heart and language. For in this dance the people do not move. Desire moves. Eros is a verb. (Carson 16–17)

Wild, too, becomes a verb.

When Thoreau says, "Give me a wildness whose glance no civilization can endure" ("Walking" 665), he is invoking the glance of Eros. Thoreau the lover is triangulating on the beloved, Nature, and the space that opens up between them—what he calls "the wild"—is the topos of his imagination. In this sense, his pursuit—his pilgrimage—reflects that of the men Socrates describes in the *Phaedrus* , each seeking his own god:

> And if they have not aforetime trodden this path, they now set out upon it, learning the way from any source that may offer or finding it for themselves; and as they follow up the trace within themselves of

the nature of their own god their task is made easier, inasmuch as they are constrained to fix their gaze upon him; and reaching out after him in memory they are possessed by him, and from him they take their ways and manners of life, in so far as a man can partake of a god. But all this, mark you, they attribute to the beloved, and the draughts which they draw from Zeus they pour out, like Bacchants, into the soul of the beloved, thus creating in him the closest possible likeness to the god they worship. (252e–253b)

"All nature is my bride," Thoreau announces in an 1857 *Journal* entry. "That nature which to one is stark and ghastly solitude is a sweet, tender, and genial society to another" (J:ix 337). Elsewhere, he writes: "Nature must be viewed humanly to be viewed at all; that is, her scenes must be associated with humane affections, such as are associated with one's native place, for instance. She is most significant to a lover. A lover of Nature is preeminently a lover of man. If I have no friend, what is Nature to me? She ceases to be morally significant" (J:iv 163). Thoreau's love for Nature is predicated on knowing how to love a fellow human being.

In pouring out his love for Nature, he is really tracing the nature of his own god, the one that props him; in short, he is seeking self. In finding self, the human being finds the world. Such a quest, by its very nature, is erotic. Aristotle says, "All men by nature desire to know." "Know thyself" is Socrates's oracular advice. If we accept the English verb "to know" with its full complement of erotic connotation, we may say "to know is to love"—both embody a reaching across the distance that separates the known from the unknown. There is a necessary narcissism implicit in this formulation, but, as such, it constitutes the primary activity of the imagination: You cannot truly love the other until you love yourself. Thoreau's love of Nature needs to be understood in this context.

As he explains in a letter to Harrison Blake: "Whether he sleeps or wakes, whether he runs or walks, whether he uses a microscope or a telescope, or his naked eye, a man never discovers anything, never overtakes anything or leaves anything behind, but himself. Whatever he says or does he merely reports himself. If he is in love, he *loves*; if he is in heaven he *enjoys*, if he is in hell he *suffers*. It is his condition that determines his locality" (*Corr* 579). The emphasis he lays on the verbs in this passage highlights the kinetic quality of the imagination that Thoreau recognizes as Eros. Nature is not the issue, but Thoreau's *love for it* is. "Nature has no outline," William Blake penned in one of his notebooks, "but Imagination has." The pilgrim's path, though it may lead through nature, arrives finally at a conception of the self. "Every man thus *tracks himself* through life, in all his hearing and reading and observation and travelling" (J:xiii 77).

Aristotle says, in the *Rhetoric*, "Pleasure is a certain motion of the soul" (1369b). That motion (*kinesis*) corresponds to the activity of the imagination as Thoreau conceives it, reaching across the gulf between known and unknown, traversing the distance, "walking" through erotic space. "Two or three hours' walking," he writes, "will carry me to as strange a country as I expect ever to see" ("Walking" 660). The imagination's walking, at least to one traveling with a pure mind, parallels the body's walking: "We would fain take that walk, never yet taken by us through this actual world, which is perfectly symbolical to us of the path which we love to travel in the interior and ideal world; and sometimes, no doubt, we find it difficult to choose our direction, because it does not yet exist in our idea" ("Walking" 662). The walking is what is important, not the destination; the pilgrimage, not the shrine. There is no "self" per se, just the "coming to know." This is Thoreau's practice of life, and in this ateleological sense he is decidedly un-Aristotelian.

In coming to know himself through the *walking* of the imagination, Thoreau prepares himself to front the fact of the Other, to perceive it in all its *Other*-ness: Boundaries dissolve, but distance remains. (Herein, we may glean some insight from the colloquial expression "The same but different.") The *Journal* entry for November 30, 1858, concerning his "discovery" of a bream in Walden Pond, amply illustrates this form of perception:

> I cannot but see still in my mind's eye those little striped breams poised in Walden's glaucous water. They balance all the rest of the world in my estimation at present, for this is the bream that I have just found, and for the time I neglect all its brethren and am ready to kill the fatted calf on its account. For more than two centuries have men fished here and have not distinguished this permanent settler of the township. It is not like a new bird, a transient visitor that may

not be seen again for years, but there it dwells and has dwelt perma-
nently, who can tell for how long? When my eyes first rested on
Walden the striped bream was poised in it, though I did not see it,
and when Tahatawan paddled his canoe there. How wild it makes
the pond and the township to find a new fish in it! America renews
her youth here. But in my account of this bream I cannot go a hair's
breadth beyond the mere statement that it exists,—the miracle of its
existence, my contemporary and neighbor, yet so different from me! I
can only poise my thought there by its side and try to think like a
bream for a moment. I can only think of precious jewels, of music,
poetry, beauty, and the mystery of life. I only see the bream in its
orbit, as I see a star, but I care not to measure its distance or weight.
The bream, appreciated, floats in the pond as the centre of the system, another image of God. Its life no man can explain more than he
can his own. I want you to perceive the mystery of the bream. I have
a contemporary in Walden. It has fins where I have legs and arms. I
have a friend among the fishes, at least a new acquaintance. Its character will interest me, I trust, not its clothes and anatomy. I do not
want it to eat. Acquaintance with it is to make my life more rich and
eventful. It is as if a poet or an anchorite had moved into the town,
whom I can see from time to time and think of yet oftener. Perhaps
there are a thousand of these striped bream which no one had
thought of in that pond,—not their mere impressions in stone, but in
the full tide of the bream life. (J:xi 358–59)

Through the medium of words, Thoreau asserts that words will not
suffice to convey anyone's genuine experience; words will not
allow him to go "a hair's breadth beyond the mere statement that
it exists." When he tries to think like a bream, the precious jewels,
music, poetry, beauty, and mystery that come to his mind are not
"the bream thinking," but the *human* thinking in terms of symbols;
the words he uses are themselves symbols. Walking becomes important because it may bring one to the "proper source." Those
who say they can think like a bream are, in fact, merely humans
*trying* to think like a bream; this is what John Ruskin called the
"pathetic fallacy." Thus, Thoreau's "thinking" remains human—
there is no other way. "Do not all strange sounds thrill us as
*human*," he says in the *Journal*, "till we have learned to refer them
to their proper source?" (J:vii 12).

Had he had access to writings of the Japanese philosopher Dōgen, Thoreau would have smiled when he found sentences like "Water's freedom depends only on water."[3] The question Dōgen poses is: If one sees the bream's thinking as a "precious jewel," does one, then, when beholding a precious jewel, see a bream thinking? Thoreau poses the same question. "I want you to perceive the mystery of the bream," he says, but (he seems to say) you will not do so through my words, or anybody else's for that matter. Both Dōgen and Thoreau are cutting to the quick of language: Since it is by nature symbolic—that is, substituting one thing for another—it is never adequate to the task of conveying our experience. Words will not pinch-hit for life. "My life is the poem I would have writ, / But I could not both live and utter it," runs Thoreau's best-known epigram. The insight he frames in all but words is that language is an outrageous catachresis (in Latin it is called *abusio*); a vast system of inappropriate substitutions. "The beauty of the fish, that is what it is best worth the while to measure. Its place in our systems is of comparatively little importance" (J:xi 360). To front a fact—whether it be a bream or a mountain—and perceive "ITS" mystery, requires the long walk, the long work of love.

---

3. "Mountains and Waters Sutra," in *Moon in a Dewdrop: Writings of Zen Master Dōgen* (102). The first three paragraphs in Section 12 are very much to the point here:

"All beings do not see mountains and waters in the same way. Some beings see water as jeweled ornament, but they do not regard jeweled ornaments as water. What in the human realm corresponds to their water? We only see their jeweled ornaments as water.

"Some beings see water as wondrous blossoms, but they do not use blossoms as water. Hungry ghosts see water as raging fire or pus and blood. Dragons see water as a palace or a pavilion. Some beings see water as a forest or a wall. Some see it as the dharma nature of pure liberation, the true human body, or as the form of body and essence of mind. Human beings see water as water. Water is seen as dead or alive depending on causes and conditions.

"Thus the view of all beings are not the same. You should question this matter now. Are there many ways to see one thing, or is it a mistake to see many forms as one thing? You should pursue this beyond the limit of pursuit. Accordingly, endeavors in practice-realization of the way are not limited to one or two kinds. The ultimate realm has one thousand kinds and ten thousand ways."

## The Work of the Mountains

I would now like to front what is perhaps the most inadequately understood passage in all of Thoreau's writing—the "Burnt Lands" section in his "Ktaadn" essay. Here is the paragraph in full:

Perhaps I most fully realized that this was primeval, untamed, and forever untameable *Nature,* or whatever else men call it, while coming down this part of the mountain. We were passing over "Burnt Lands," burnt by lightning, perchance, though they showed no recent marks of fire, hardly so much as a charred stump, but looked rather like a natural pasture for the moose and deer, exceedingly wild and desolate, with occasional strips of timber crossing them, and low poplars springing up, and patches of blueberries here and there. I found myself traversing them familiarly, like some pasture run to waste, or partially reclaimed by man; but when I reflected what man, what brother or sister or kinsman of our race made it and claimed it, I expected the proprietor to rise up and dispute my passage. It is difficult to conceive of a region uninhabited by man. We habitually presume his presence and influence everywhere. And yet we have not seen pure Nature, unless we have seen her thus vast, and drear, and inhuman, though in the midst of cities. Nature was here something savage and awful, though beautiful. I looked with awe at the ground I trod on, to see what the Powers had made there, the form and fashion and material of their work. This was the Earth of which we have heard, made out of Chaos and Old Night. Here was no man's garden, but the unhandselled globe. It was not lawn, nor pasture, nor mead, nor woodland, nor lea, nor arable, nor waste-land. It was the fresh and natural surface of the planet Earth, as it was made forever and ever,—to be the dwelling of man, we say,—so Nature made it, and man may use it if he can. Man was not to be associated with it. It was Matter, vast, terrific,—not his Mother Earth that we have heard of, not for him to tread on, or to be buried in,—no, it were being too familiar even to let his bones lie there—the home of Necessity and Fate. There was there felt the presence of a force not bound to be kind to man. It was a place for heathenism and superstitious rites,—to be inhabited by men nearer of kin to the rocks and to wild animals than we. We walked over it with a certain awe, stopping from time to time to pick the blueberries which grew there, and had a smart and spicy taste. Perchance where *our* wild pines stand, and leaves lie on their forest floor in Concord, there were once reapers, and husbandmen planted grain; but here not even the surface had been scarred by man, but it was a specimen of what God saw fit to make this world. What is it to be admitted to a museum, to see a myriad of particular things, compared with being shown some star's surface, some hard matter in its home! I stand in awe of my body, this matter to which I am bound has become so strange to me. I fear not spirits, ghosts, of which I am one,—*that* my body might,—but I fear bodies, I tremble to meet them. What is this Titan that has possession of me? Talk of mysteries!—Think of our life in nature,—daily to be shown matter, to come in contact with it,—rocks, trees, wind on our cheeks! the *solid* earth! the *actual* world! the *common sense! Contact! Contact! Who* are we? *where* are we? (*Maine Woods* 69–71)

The "standard" interpretation of the passage runs something like this: "This experience at Katahdin so alarmed and unhinged him that in 'Katahdin' [*sic*] he appears to be momentarily unbalanced and uncharacteristically out of control. . . . Thoreau is not only alienated from nature but is also beside himself; the Katahdin episode clearly terrified and disoriented him. . . . The Maine woods, the real woods as opposed to Walden's, were intractable to human molding, imaginatively unmalleable and impenetrable" (Lebeaux 56).[4] An argument such as this is tenable only in a narrow (Thoreau would say "common-sense") context, possible only if the reader denies the numerous, obvious counters to it in the text, not the least of which is the tone, which is not one of "terror" but of *awe* (he uses this word or its variant four times). In the context of Thoreau's discipline of pure mind, this passage is not only thoroughly consistent with his practice, but further aids us in understanding that practice.

To return once more to Dōgen, to the end of the "Mountains and Waters Sutra": "There are mountains hidden in treasures.

---

4. Although I am quoting Lebeaux's words, they are representative of a whole lineage of Thoreau commentators, from Leo Stoller (*After Walden*) through Leo Marx (*The Machine in the Garden*) and down to the present. For a thorough genealogy of this scholarly interpretation, see Stephen Adams and Donald Ross, Jr., *Revising Mythologies: The Composition of Thoreau's Major Works.* All of this calls to mind a pertinent passage from Thoreau's *Journal*: "It is necessary to find out exactly what books to read on a given subject. Though there may be a thousand books written upon it, it is only important to read three or four; they will contain all that is essential, and a few pages will show you which they are. Books which are books are all that you want, and there are but half a dozen in any thousand" (J:iii 353).

There are mountains hidden in swamps. There are mountains hidden in the sky. There are mountains hidden in mountains. There are mountains hidden in hiddenness. This is complete understanding." I offer Dōgen here as a guide, one who points to "fresh woods and pastures new" (to use one of Thoreau's favorite lines from Milton). "When you investigate mountains thoroughly," the penultimate line of the sutra runs: "this is the work of the mountains" (107). Mountains, after all, provided Thoreau with some of the most powerful imagery in his prose; mountains also dominated the landscape of his dreams.

A substantial portion of the *Journal* passage for October 29, 1857, is devoted to giving an account of a recurring dream ("for the twentieth time at least"), which he only now remembers; it is a dream about a mountain. Lying in the eastern part of Concord ("where no high hill actually is"), Thoreau attempts to describe it:

> My way up used to lie through a dark and unfrequented wood at its base,—I cannot now tell exactly, it was so long ago, under what circumstances I first ascended, only that I shuddered as I went along (I have an indistinct remembrance of having been out overnight alone),—and then I steadily ascended along a rocky ridge half clad with stinted trees, where wild beasts haunted, till I lost myself quite in the upper air and clouds, seeming to pass an imaginary line which separates a hill, mere earth heaped up, from a mountain, into a superterranean grandeur and sublimity. What distinguishes that summit above the earthy line, is that it is unhandselled, awful, grand. It can never become familiar; you are lost the moment you set foot there. You know the path, but wander, thrilled, over the bare and pathless rock, as if it were solidified air and cloud. That rocky, misty summit, secreted in the clouds, was far more thrillingly awful and sublime than the crater of a volcano spouting fire. (J:x 142)

This passage, written eleven years after Thoreau's first trip to Maine, bears comparison to the "Ktaadn" essay; the choice of words to describe his "alpine" experience is identical.[5] Both are in-

---

5. In a letter to Harrison Blake, he relates: "I keep a mountain anchored off eastward a little way, which I ascend in my dreams both awake and asleep. Its broad base spreads over a village or two, which do not know it; neither does it know them, nor do I when I ascend it. I can see its general outline as plainly now in my mind as that of Wachusett. I do not invent in the least, but state exactly

fused with that sense of awe. When Thoreau says he "shuddered" as he went along, he means the sort of trembling that accompanies goose bumps, the kind that one feels in the presence of the beloved. This trembling occurs as he crosses the limen ("an imaginary line") and enters the erotic space wherein he loses himself; it is a region that is "unhandselled, awful, grand" (the "Burnt Lands" are "the unhandselled globe"). The loss of self is a terrifying experience, no doubt, but it is a necessary terror, a prelude to enlightenment. In "Ktaadn," he writes: "Some part of the beholder, even some vital part, seems to escape through the loose grating of his ribs as he ascends. He is more lone than you can imagine. . . . His reason is dispersed and shadowy, more thin and subtile like the air. Vast, Titanic, inhuman Nature has got him at disadvantage, caught him alone, and pilfers him of some of his divine faculty." The divine faculty, in this case, is the ego's dependence upon reason; denied this, one is simply mad. Thoreau's description of his experience on Mount Katahdin is thus analogous to that of a lover. In the dream mountain passage, he writes: "This is a business we can partly understand. The perfect mountain height is already thoroughly purified. It is as if you trod with awe the face of a god turned up." In fact, he describes the cloud-shrouded summit of this dream mountain as "a hard-featured god reposing, whose breath hangs about his forehead." The god, it would seem, is Eros.

Eros hovers over every pilgrim, and Thoreau—a pilgrim who climbs mountains both in his waking moments and in his dreams—concludes: "Though the *pleasure* of ascending the mountain is largely mixed with awe, my thoughts are purified and sublimed by it, as if I had been translated" (emphasis added). The translation is one of consciousness—*satori*, as Zen Buddhists would have it—from the common sense to pure mind. The same sort of translation, complete with the contradictory feelings, informs the "Ktaadn" essay: "Nature here was something savage and awful, though beautiful." He is caught in the wild glance of Eros. The important lesson for the pilgrim is to recognize that Eros himself in-

---

what I see. I find that I go up it when I am light-footed and earnest. It ever smokes like an altar with its sacrifice. I am not aware that a single villager frequents it or knows of it. I keep this mountain to ride instead of a horse" (*Corr* 498).

habits an *inhuman* realm, that ultimately this site is not to be colonized—it remains forever wild. "It is difficult to conceive of a region uninhabited by man," Thoreau writes, but here it is—and the pilgrim, afforded a mere glimpse (even this inadequate) must go home. "[I]t is good collyrium to look on the bare earth," he writes elsewhere, perhaps recalling his dream mountain or Katahdin itself, "to pore over it so much, getting strength for all your senses, like Antaeus" (J:xii 89). The two worlds—home and the wild "away"—though vastly different, are, in fact, one. "I do believe," he writes in his first letter to Harrison Blake, "that the outward and the inward life correspond; that if any should succeed to live a higher life, others would not know of it; that difference and distance are one" (*Corr* 214). This is an enantiodromic knowledge of the edge—it finds an analogue in the account of the dream mountain:

> There are ever two ways up: one is through the dark wood, the other through the sunny pasture. That is, I reach and discover the mountain only through the dark wood, but I see to my surprise, when I look off between the mists from the summit, how it is ever adjacent to my native fields, nay, imminent over them, and accessible through a sunny pasture. Why is it that in the lives of men we hear more of the dark wood than of the sunny pasture? (J:x 143)

The pilgrim, the mountain climber, makes the long journey only to find that heaven is at home, residing in the self.[6] In terms of perception, the sunny pasture is the phenomenal world replete with its mere "suchness." As the poet Lew Welch phrases it: "*This is the last place. / There is nowhere else we need to go*" (*Ring of Bone* 122).

No doubt Thoreau's experience on Mount Katahdin had a profound effect upon him, but it is not one of cowardly retreat to the pastoral, humanized landscape of Concord, as many non-mountain-climbing scholars would have it. The last several sentences of the Burnt Lands passage do show that Thoreau's philosophy of

---

6. Thoreau concludes his account of the dream mountain with a poem, whose last four lines are: "It is a spiral path within the pilgrim's soul / Leads to this mountain's brow; / commencing at his hearth he climbs up to this goal / He knows not when or how."

Transcendentalism was shaken up—by a confrontation with the *matter* that is his body. He is forced here to admit that even Transcendentalists have bodies. Thoreau, more often than not, privileges the mind over the body, the ideal over the actual. The real shock for him coming down from Katahdin is that his body is made from the same matter that this unhandselled wilderness is— *that his body is wild.* In his privileging of the mind, he had forgotten he has a body. "I stand in awe of my body, this matter to which I am bound has become so strange to me." He tells us he doesn't fear spirits or ghosts because they are of the mind, and can be apprehended as such. Bodies, on the other hand, can only be understood by other bodies. Thoreau is startled into awareness that the body has its own way of "thinking," not conducted through words— here, it is "hard matter in its home." Despite the gulf that will not be bridged by language, he intuits the mind and body are one, providing him with a shock of recognition. "Talk of mysteries!— Think of our life in nature,—daily to be shown matter, to come in contact with it, rocks, trees, wind on our cheeks! the *solid* earth! the *actual* world!" He realizes that even the common sense he so disparages has its intrinsic worth, its suchness; it, too, is part of the "*actual*."[7] "*Contact! Contact!*" is the cry of the liminar in the midst

---

7. This is not to say that Thoreau ever fully reconciled himself to the common sense; let us just say he better understood it. As to the "suchness" of things, that which cannot be framed in words ("I do not know of any poetry to quote which adequately expresses this yearning for the Wild" ["Walking" 668]), he continued to insist that such perception was more than "fact" alone. A few years later, he writes in his *Journal:* "I, too, would fain set down something besides facts. Facts should only be as the frame to my pictures; they should be material to the mythology which I am writing; not facts to assist men to make money, farmers to farm profitably, in any common sense; facts to tell who I am, and where I have been or what I have thought: as now the bell rings for evening meeting, and its volumes of sound, like smoke which rises from where a cannon is fired, make the tent in which I dwell. My facts shall be falsehoods to the common sense. I would so state facts that they shall be significant, shall be myths or mythologic. Facts which the mind perceived, thoughts which the body thought,—with these I deal. I, too, cherish vague and misty forms, vaguest when the cloud at which I gaze is dissipated quite and naught but the skyey depths are seen" (J:iii 99). In "Walking," after expressing his longing for a poetry of the Wild, he says: "Mythology comes nearer to it than anything. How much more fertile a Nature, at least, has Grecian mythology its root than English literature! Mythology is the crop which the Old World bore before its soil was exhausted" (668).

of erotic space, who witnesses the dissolution of boundaries between mind and body. In "Walking," he expresses it: "For my part, I feel that with regard to Nature I live a sort of border life, on the confines of a world into which I make occasional and transient forays only, and my patriotism and allegiance to the State into whose territories I seem to retreat are those of a moss-trooper" ("Walking" 672). This is Thoreau's work of the mountains.

### Sympathy with Intelligence

To return to "Walking" and to conclude this saunter where we began, it is useful to reiterate the goal of Thoreau's practice: a disciplined un-learning, an active dismantling of what the common sense refers to as "knowledge," leads not to nihilism, but to wisdom. "My desire for knowledge is intermittent; but my desire to bathe my head in atmospheres unknown to my feet is perennial and constant. The highest that we can attain to is not Knowledge, but Sympathy with Intelligence. . . . It is the lighting up of the mist by the sun. Man cannot *know* in any higher sense than this" (671). The work of the mountains dominates his late philosophical letters to Harrison Blake, letters wherein he recapitulates the lessons of a mountain-climbing life.

In an 1857 letter, Thoreau writes a paragraph that could well serve as a gloss to the Burnt Lands passage in "Ktaadn":

> You must have been enriched by your solitary walk over the mountains. I suppose that I feel the same awe when on their summits that many do on entering a church. To see what kind of earth that is on which you have a house and garden somewhere, perchance! It is equal to the lapse of many years. You must ascend a mountain to learn your relation to matter, and so to your own body, for *it* is at home there, though *you* are not. It might have been composed there, and will have no farther to go to return to dust there, than in your garden; but your spirit inevitably comes away, and brings your body with it, if it lives. Just as awful really, and as glorious, as your garden. See how I can play with my fingers! They are the funniest companions I have ever found. Where did they come from? What strange control I have over them! *Who* am I? What are they?—those little peaks—call them Madison, Jefferson, Lafayette. What is the *matter*?

My fingers ten, I say. Why, erelong, they may form the top-most crystal of Mount Washington. I go up there to see my body's cousins. There are some fingers, toes, bowels, etc., that I take an interest in, and therefore I am interested in all their relations. (*Corr* 497)

Even though he never seems to "overcome" the difference between mind and body, he is very much aware of this difference, and is amazed by it; he stands in the midst of it, this erotic space, and watches the free play of the imagination. Mountains are bodies; bodies are mountains; his fingers become a Presidential Range. In an 1860 letter, Thoreau's ethic, steeped in high mountains, emerges once again:

The snow-clad summit of Mt. Washington must have been a very interesting sight from Wachusett. How wholesome winter is seen far or near, how good above all mere sentimental warm-blooded—short-lived, soft-hearted *moral* goodness, commonly so called. Give me the goodness which has forgotten its own deeds,—which God has seen to be good and let be. None of your *just made perfect*—pickled eels! All that will save them will be their picturesqueness, as with blasted trees [sic] Whatever is and is not ashamed to be is good. I value no moral goodness or greatness unless it is good or great as that snowy peak is. Pray how could thirty feet of bowels improve it? Nature is goodness crystalized. You looked into the land of promise. Whatever beauty we behold, the more it is distant, serene, and cold, the purer & more durable it is. It is better to warm ourselves with ice than with fire. (*Corr* 598)

Thoreau, as he so often does, casts a cold eye on common-sense morality. When he asks Blake in another letter, "What mountain are you camping on nowadays?" he is posing an ethical question.

Herein lies Thoreau's lesson of pilgrimage: "To let the mountains slide,—live at home like a traveler. It should not be in vain that these things are shown to us from day to day. Is not each withered leaf that I see in my walks something which I have traveled to find?—traveled, who can tell how far? What a fool he must be who thinks El Dorado is anywhere but where he lives!" (*Corr* 538). Pilgrimage is an attitude, what the pilgrim brings home. "Where is the 'Unexplored land' but in our own untried enterprises?" Thoreau asks, not only of Harrison Blake but of all his readers:

> To an adventurous spirit any place,—London New York, Worcester,
> or his own yard, is 'unexplored land,' to seek which Fremont & Kane
> travel so far. To a sluggish and defeated spirit even the Great Basin &
> the Polaris are trivial places. If ever they get there (& indeed they are
> there now) they will want to sleep & give it up, just as they always do.
> What is the use of going over the old track again? There is an adder
> in the path which your own feet have worn. You must make tracks
> into the Unknown. That is what you have your board & clothes for.
> Why do you ever mend your clothes, unless that, wearing them, you
> may mend your ways? (*Corr* 580)

The pilgrim must not "fall asleep" and thereby "give up" the insight gained by crossing the threshold between Known and Unknown. As he says in the sentence he finally chose as the epigraph
for *Walden*, the pilgrim must "brag as lustily as chanticleer in the
morning, if only to wake my neighbors up." Or, as he expresses it
in "Walking": "Above all, we cannot afford not to live in the present. . . . It is an expression of the health and soundness of Nature,
a brag for all the world,—healthiness as of a spring burst forth, a
new fountain of the Muses, to celebrate this last instant of time"
(673). Sauntering, in the end, is all a work of love.

THREE

# John Muir's Parables of Desire

> A light breeze rustles the reeds
> Along the river banks. The
> Mast of my lonely boat soars
> Into the night. Stars blossom
> Over the vast desert of
> Waters. Moonlight flows on the
> Surging river. My poems have
> Made me famous but I grow
> Old, ill and tired, blown hither
> And yon; I am like a gull
> Lost between heaven and earth.
> —Tu Fu, translated by Kenneth Rexroth

### "John of the Rivers"

The story of John Muir begins with a walk. On September 1, 1867, when he was twenty-nine years old, he started out from Indianapolis. His plan: "simply to push on in a general southward direction by the wildest, leafiest, and least trodden way I could find, promising the greatest extent of virgin forest" (TMW 1–2). This walk, though not his first, did break the orbit of home, inaugurating a ten-year pilgrimage to the wild. Although this particular excursion came to an abrupt halt in malarial fever on the Gulf Coast of Florida, it was followed by two months of recovery, a sojourn in Cuba, and then, a springtime arrival by ship in San Francisco, where, so the story goes, John Muir stopped a man on the street and asked the quickest way out of the city. "But where do you want to go?" the man asked. "Anywhere that is wild," Muir replied, and was promptly pointed eastward toward the Oakland ferry. There, in the California distance, lay the range of light-soaked mountains that would make him famous.

"John of the Mountains," as he came to be known—John Muir walking, climbing, pursuing his desire, to-ing and fro-ing the length and breadth of California, singing its undomesticated praises. He, more than anyone else, is our wilderness warbler, and radiating from his writings is that tremendous great joy of discovering and exploring the body and soul of the beloved. Like Thoreau before him (whose writings he could recite) and Ruess after him, Muir walks his way into our memory. Ten years of walking, ten years of pilgrim wanderings, now in the golden foothills, now in Yosemite Valley, now in the High Sierra, now in the Bay Area, now "Shastaward" among "dead rivers," now—at last—floating down the San Joaquin River to the place that would become his home. For ten years, a peripatetic lover of storms and cascades, a vagabond adrift in vague streams, an "ambitious amateur" geologist who, slipping along the margins of civilization, did not seek the traces of gold and silver, but those of glacier and ancient river.[1] John Muir's great discovery: "Out here in the free and unplanted fields there is no rectilineal sectioning of time and seasons. All things *flow* here in indivisible, measureless currents" (JOM 8).

Muir did not publish a book until he was fifty-six years old, but by the time *The Mountains of California* appeared in 1894, readers already knew him as the author of numerous wilderness sketches and essays that had appeared in periodicals during the 1870s.[2] This first book was largely a knitting together of those earlier writings; indeed, the bulk of Muir's published work in the last twenty years of his life—the books upon which his literary and environmental reputation rests—is derived substantially from revision of sketches, essays, letters, and journal entries originally composed between 1867 and 1877. His best writings are those he penned while on the edge, while he was a liminar, while he traversed that frontier between civilization and the wild. These essays, letters, and journal entries are his parables of desire.

The best known of these parables recounts the story of his climb of Mount Ritter, and though this narrative appears as a chapter in *The Mountains of California* entitled "A Near View of the High Sierra," it was first published in *Scribner's Monthly* as "In the Heart of the California Alps." Although the events in this essay take place in 1872, Muir did not get around to putting them

---

1. The epithet "ambitious amateur" comes from Clarence King. See *Systematic Geology* (478n.).

2. In the 1880s, Muir also edited a collection of travel essays, some of which he authored himself. See *Picturesque California*.

into prose until the late 1870s, after his pilgrim years had drawn to a close. Nevertheless, the text is representative of his decade of wandering, and it even offers an apologia of sorts for the relentless pursuit of his bliss: "But we little know until tried how much of the uncontrollable there is in us, urging across glaciers and torrents, and up dangerous heights, let the judgement forbid as it may" (349). The "uncontrollable" of which he speaks is the unnameable wild. On the same trail as Thoreau, Muir suggests that, though linguistically unframeable, the wild may be *walked through*. Such wild walking requires a commitment, "the love-work of a whole life" (345), as Muir tells us. Commentators on this narrative inevitably focus on the actual details of Muir's ascent of the peak, especially the moment when, on an airy exposure, he suddenly realizes: "My doom appeared fixed. I must fall," but then, "life blazed forth again with preternatural clearness," and he became "possessed of a new sense. The other self—the ghost of by-gone experiences, Instinct or Guardian Angel—call it what you will—came forward and assumed control" (350). This is a noteworthy episode in the context of mountaineering literature, but it is less instructive about the "love-work" of Muir's life.

Far more typical of his writerly attention—what he himself is most interested in—are those portions of the essay (constituting the bulk of it) that describe his journeying to and from the mountain, in "so wild and so beautiful a region" where "every sight and sound" was "inspiring, leading one far out of oneself, yet feeding and building a strict individuality" (347). This is the pilgrim Muir, chronicler of liminality, love-maker to the flows. He encounters Eros on this Ritter excursion, as he so often does, in the form of a mountain stream:

> All my first day was pure pleasure; crossing the dry pathways of the grand old glaciers, tracing happy streams, and learning the habits of the birds and marmots in the groves and rocks. Before I had gone a mile from camp, I came to the foot of a white cascade that beats its way down a rugged gorge in the cañon wall, from a height of about nine hundred feet, and pours its throbbing waters into the Tuolumne. I was acquainted with its fountains, which, fortunately, lay in my course. What a fine traveling companion it proved to be, what songs it sang, and how passionately it told the mountain's own joy! (347)

The writer Muir is intoxicated with the Heraclitean elixir of water imagery; the Sierra Nevada streams through the alembic of his prose: "Westward the general flank of the range is seen flowing sublimely away from the sharp summits, in smooth undulations; a sea of gray granite waves dotted with lakes and meadows, and fluted with stupendous cañons that grow steadily deeper as they receded in the distance" (350).

Although it is commonplace to associate Muir with the "mountains," his most vivid writing surges in loving description of rivers and streams. "John of the Mountains" is the later John Muir, the environmental prophet howling from the wilderness; whereas the early John Muir, the John Muir who took Emerson at his word (viz.,"The world thus exists to the soul to satisfy the desire for beauty"), is more aptly known as "John of the Rivers." This is the writer John Muir who relentlessly pursues the question: Where do we find the language for what we love? This is the John Muir who begins his ten-year pilgrimage with a walk—and concludes it with a float down the San Joaquin River.

### The First Three Decades

John Muir was born in Dunbar, Scotland, in 1838. When he was eleven years old, his family moved to North America to establish a pioneer farm in Wisconsin, where he remained with the family on the farm until 1860, when he embarked on his earliest peregrinations and made his way to the Wisconsin State Agricultural Fair in Madison. Here, he displayed a number of his "inventions," including an "early-rising machine," a sort of alarm-clock bed that literally tossed its sleeper out of the sheets at the appointed time.[3] For this, he was awarded a prize and attracted a significant share of attention, most importantly from Jeanne Carr, wife of a university professor; she was to become a most profound influence on his emotional life and literary career.

---

3. Commentators on Muir's life emphasize the humor easily found in such an invention, but we should note that Muir himself apparently fashioned this contraption without any sense of irony. Some have suggested the early-rising machine reflects the early Muir's Puritan work ethic; I would add that it also reflects Muir's anxiety over the bed as a playground of potential Eros.

A second important influence asserted itself in the waning months of 1860, in Prairie du Chien, Wisconsin, where Muir befriended Emily Pelton, niece of the hotelkeeper for whom he worked part time. In joining him on many a companionable walk along the Wisconsin River, she became his first romantic love, "John's girl" (as his sister Sarah and her husband, David Galloway, referred to her), a significant rapid in the current of his desire. Muir, it would appear, was emotionally ill equipped for this encounter. The hotel where Emily lived with her relatives was the center of the town's social life, a place where the "young folks danced, and even indulged in kissing games." Muir, we are told, "was terribly shocked at first" by such wantonness (Wolfe, *Son of the Wilderness* 62). In a rebuke he delivered one evening to a room full of merrymakers, chastising them for "worldliness and silly talk," we find reason to suspect his words are directed more at himself than at anybody else, an effort to repress whatever swells of Eros were rising in him. Though he was laughed out of the room by the revelers, he recomposed his jitters into a fiery denunciation that he promptly sent off as a letter to his sister Sarah and her husband. So intense was this diatribe against innocent desire, David Galloway made a special trip to Prairie du Chien just to calm his discombobulated brother-in-law. Years later, writing to Emily from Yosemite, Muir recalled the incident with embarrassment: "Something or other jostled a bunch of the old Mondell memories. I thought of the days when I came in fresh verdure from the Wisconsin woods, and when I used to hurl very orthodox denunciations at all things morally or religiously amiss in old or young. It appears strange to me that you should all have been so patient with me" (63). By this point, his intolerance had been tempered by the loneliness of his pilgrim years.

In January 1861, Muir enrolled at the University of Wisconsin, where he remained on and off for the next two years in a perpetual state of anxiety due, in part, to thoughts of the Civil War and fears of being drafted, but perhaps equally due to his young adult restlessness. One friend described him at this time as "a storage battery of energy, encased in flexible, elastic steel" (qtd. in Wolfe, *Son of the Wilderness* 83). This energy, its flow, was desire itself seeking its channel in Muir's life. It is not surprising, then, that we should

find him, after leaving the university and embarking on an exploration of the Wisconsin River, calling in on the Peltons in Prairie
du Chien, strolling once again with Emily along the river, where
"finding comfort—even joy—in each other's companionship, it
would have been easy for him to speak words to the lonely girl that
would have joined their lives henceforth" (85). But Muir, it would
seem, spoke no such words, and he resumed his explorations down
the river. On his return trip, however, feeling lonely, he stopped
again at the Peltons, only to be turned away at the door by Emily's
uncle, who told him that she was not at home. Later, he learned
that she *was* at home. Muir was puzzled by this rebuff, but he may
have broken the "lonely" Emily's heart on those earlier river
walks—by *not* proposing marriage to her, and, instead, following
his desire *down the river*. The perceptive Emily had already recognized Muir's "true love," and in her refusal to see him we can believe that she was protecting herself. Despite this turn of events,
the two were destined to resume their relationship in California.

The next few years of Muir's life were characterized by an aimless migration (though perhaps tinged with an element of draft
dodging) around the upper Midwest and lower Canada—botany
expeditions punctuated by factory jobs, the last one at a carriage
plant in Indianapolis, where he suffered an eye injury that induced
temporary blindness. Following the recovery of his eyesight, he de-
cided to commit his life and love to the study of nature. In September 1867, he embarked on his thousand-mile walk.

### The Early Pilgrim Years

"I wish I knew where I was going," Muir wrote to Jeanne
Carr two days before his departure. "Doomed to be 'carried of the
spirit into the wilderness,' I suppose. I wish I could be more moder-
ate in my desires, but I cannot, and so there is no rest" (LF 32).
The same immoderation whelmed in Bunyan's Christian, who—
with his fingers plugged in his ears to avoid hearing his wife and
children crying after him—ran away from home into the wilderness, shouting "Life, life, eternal life" (Bunyan 19). Emily Pelton,
for one, would have recognized this correspondence.

The walk—as in "I'm going for a walk"—carries the body off into unfamiliar space, away from habit (and perhaps despair) into surprise; distance is bred with time into movement. Such was the urge behind the earliest historical examples of pilgrimage—the desire simply to walk away. This is also the basis of the quest motif—which, in effect, is a *pursuit*—but the word *quest* directs attention to a distant and often material goal rather than to the process of the journey, the simple joy inherent in it. Whereas a quest narrative corresponds to what Stanley Fish has identified as a "rhetorical presentation"—that is, a rhetorical form that mirrors for approval "the opinions its readers already hold"—the pilgrim's narrative is "dialectical," indeed *disturbing*, "for it requires of its readers a searching and rigorous scrutiny of everything they believe in and live by" (1).[4] William LaFleur points to the same process-based understanding in the Japanese Buddhist tradition, where "the goal of pilgrimage is often found within the natural world through which the pilgrim-poet travels rather than at some distant place deemed and designated as 'sacred' by the consensus of the cultus-concerned religious community" (Callicott 198). The pilgrim self awakes from reverie into revolution.

Thus, in the beginning there was only walking, which brought the individual directly, physically, into liminality. It was only at later points in the histories of various cultures that such walking away, such aimless wandering, such passaging, gradually came under cultural regulation, becoming institutionalized as formal pilgrimage. Pure passages were transformed into rites.[5] Muir's walk into the American wilderness, for the sheer joy of it, was relatively unmediated by cultural precedents. There were no backpacking magazines, no equipment stores, no wilderness "industry." Although he hadn't yet realized it, he, in fact, was helping to set cultural precedent in the very journal he kept of this trip,

---

4. Fish continues: "[The dialectical presentation] is didactic in a special sense; it does not preach the truth, but asks that its readers discover the truth for themselves, and this discovery is often made at the expense not only of a reader's opinions and values, but of his self-esteem. If the experience of a rhetorical form is flattering, the experience of a dialectical form is humiliating."

5. See van Gennep (*Rites of Passage*) and Victor and Edith Turner (*Image and Pilgrimage*).

which would not be published until 1916, two years after his death.[6]

The journal of Muir's thousand-mile walk, like the decade of his pilgrim years, is interspersed with moments of liminality. Recalling Victor Turner's observation that the liminal state "has frequently been likened to death" (Victor and Edith Turner 249), it is no surprise to find the narrative center of the journal located in a graveyard. By early October, Muir had reached Savannah, Georgia, but had run out of money and was awaiting more to be sent by his brother. In the meantime, on the outskirts of town, he found the Bonaventure graveyard a consoling campground: "You hear the song of birds, cross a small stream, and are with Nature in the grand old forest graveyard, so beautiful that almost any sensible person would choose to dwell here with the dead rather than with the lazy, disorderly living" (TMW 67). Muir was fully aware that his residency in a graveyard would only arouse suspicion among the townspeople; in this sense, he knew he was beyond the pale of society—that he was, in fact, an outlaw. "That I might not be observed and suspected of hiding, as if I had committed a crime, I always went home after dark" (77). In addition, he described himself as "dangerously hungry" (79). He was living among ghosts, a ghost among the living.

By the time he reached the Gulf Coast of Florida at the end of the month, Muir was on the threshold of death, suffering a malarial fever that as much surprised him ("for I never before was sick") as it overwhelmed him: "the fever broke on me like a storm, and before I staggered halfway to the mill I fell down unconscious on the narrow trail among the dwarf palmettos" (128). Given Muir's later passionate descriptions of storms, the analogy he employs here is intriguing, especially as he continues the account of his illness with the same language he would eventually apply in his most evocative passages of the natural world: "I rose, staggered, and fell,

---

6. TMW was edited by William Frederick Badé. Some might argue, Michael Cohen (*The Pathless Way*) among them, that *A Thousand-Mile Walk*, because of possible later revisions, should be regarded with suspicion if we take it as an expression of the young John Muir. I, however, follow William and Maymie Kimes (*John Muir: A Reading Bibliography*), who note: "Dr. Badé edited the journal very slightly; therefore, it retains the freshness of events as they occurred, as well as Muir's innermost thoughts as he pondered the problem of man's place in the universe" (98).

I know not how many times, in delirious bewilderment, gasping and throbbing with only moments of consciousness."[7] This liminal experience of his physical health was pivotal in the evolution of Muir's attitude toward the wild.

He recovered over the next months, made the trip to Cuba, and eventually arrived in California, where, after wandering to Yosemite via Pacheco Pass, he took a job as a shepherd near the Sierra foothill town of Snelling. Writing a few years later about this grassy, crenate lowland with its backdrop of distant peaks, Muir describes it in trademark fashion: "You can not feel yourself out-of-doors; plain, sky, and mountains ray beauty which you feel. You bathe in these spirit-beams, turning round and round, as if warming at a camp-fire. Presently you lose consciousness of your own separate existence: you blend with the landscape, and become part and parcel of Nature" ("Twenty Hill Hollow" 86). Reflecting on his experience thus far in California, he writes in his journal for December 1868: "In these walks there has been no human method—no law—no rule" (JOM 2). Despite the assurance with which he typically portrays his wild rambles in the pilgrim years, these writings pulse with an undercurrent of doubt. He concludes the above journal passage: "Such a life has been mine, every day and night of last summer spent beneath the open sky; but last month brought California winter and rain, so a roof became necessary, and the question came, What shall I do? Where shall I go?" Questions of necessity, but they also suggest a loneliness. He writes, dolefully, to Jeanne Carr on February 24, 1869: "I have not made a single friend in California" (LF 49). In this sense, his experience is not unlike that of Everett Ruess: both were lonely in the wild.

Muir nevertheless did manage to dispel—or perhaps we could say "escape"—his loneliness during the summer of 1869, when he shepherded in the mountains. "Wrote to my mother and a few friends," he tells us, "mountain hints to each. They seem as near as if within voice-reach or touch. The deeper the solitude the less the sense of loneliness, and the nearer our friends" (FS 134). Muir

---

7. The word *throbbing* is one of Muir's favorites, and he employs it frequently in descriptions of his cascade-induced ecstasies.

recorded this important season in his life in the journal that, years later and somewhat revised, he published as *My First Summer in the Sierra*. His words in this book attest that this was the summer when he fell most deeply in love, the summer when desire scoured its most impressive channels in his psyche. This rapture was projected out upon the landscape, where he saw it reflected in the glacial polish of Yosemite granite, in the sparkle of Sierra streams and cascades and waterfalls.

On July 15, Muir "rambled along the [Yosemite] valley rim," eagerly seeking exposed ledges where he would scramble out and gaze into the chasm below. "When such places were found, and I had cautiously set my feet and drawn my body erect, I could not help fearing a little that the rock might split off and let me down, and what a down!" (FS 117) He was seduced by these *petit mortes*, bringing him to the self's ecstatic edge: The brink of Yosemite Valley corresponds to an erogenous zone of his imagination. He confesses this lust: "After withdrawing from such places, excited with the view I got, I would say to myself, 'Now don't go out on the verge again.' But in the face of Yosemite scenery cautious remonstrance is vain; under its spell one's body seems to go where it likes with a will over which we seem to have scarce any control" (118).

On this walk Muir eventually reaches Yosemite Creek, where he achieves his first view from atop the falls. After "admiring its easy, graceful, confident gestures" and its "singing," he becomes infatuated by peeking in on the stream as "it seems to rest and compose its gray, agitated waters before taking the grand plunge, then slowly slipping over the lip of the pool basin, it descends another glossy slope with rapidly accelerated speed to the brink of the tremendous cliff, and with sublime, fateful confidence springs out free in the air." At last, he has recognized desire itself. His unrestrained response: "I took off my shoes and stockings and worked my way cautiously down alongside the rushing flood, keeping my feet and hands pressed firmly on the polished rock. The booming, roaring water, rushing past close to my head, was very exciting." The object of his desire is "to see the forms and behavior of the fall all the way down to the bottom," and despite "the swift roaring flood," which is "very nerve-trying," he makes his way out to a small ledge. "Here I obtained a perfectly free view down into the heart of the snowy, chanting throng of comet-like streamers, into which the body of the fall soon separates." He tells us that the "tremendous grandeur of the fall in form and sound and motion, acting at close range, smothered the sense of fear" (120). The words barely contain the exuberance: He is a lover attempting to explain to his readers the embrace of his beloved's body. Among American writers, Muir is a premier sensualist—though he is un-recognized as such because he was writing about a para-human love affair.

Muir's account of his first visit to the summit of Yosemite Falls, laden as his words are with suggestive language, reads less like a de-scription of the natural world than like a medieval knight's en-counter with "la belle dame sans merci." To render the wild with an erotic charge is characteristic of Muir's best writing. In tradi-tional "la belle dame" poems—Keats's, in particular—the land-scape becomes a metaphor for the knight's psyche, wherein he en-counters, ruefully, a feminine representation of desire. Muir, how-ever, after his encounter with la belle dame of Yosemite Creek, es-capes the postcoital blues that plague Keats's "haggard and woe-be-gone" knight. Instead, he writes with barely restrained ecstasy: "How long I remained down there, or how I returned, I can hardly tell. Anyhow I had a glorious time, and got back to camp about dark, enjoying triumphant exhilaration soon followed by dull weariness."[8] For Muir, the landscape—particularly its flowing water—always bespeaks desire.

I must interject here that my reading is not designed to reduce Muir's work to an expression of his own sexual frustration. On the contrary, my efforts are intended to open the floodgates. Muir was always attractive to women. Had he chosen—and, as we shall see, *he may indeed have chosen*—he would have had no problem in find-ing a lover or a wife. But Muir's own sense of desire, like that of Everett Ruess, Henry Thoreau, and most male writers who choose the wild as their subject, was at this time in his life too extensive to be contained in a single human body. "But we always make love with worlds," a philosopher and a psychoanalyst have co-written. "And our love addresses itself to this libidinal property of our

---

8. All quotes are drawn from FS 115–120.

lover, to either close himself off or open up to more spacious worlds, to masses and large aggregates" (Deleuze and Guattari 294). Muir was wildly and innocently making love with the world, and this more than anything else accounts for the childlike quality that is said to have radiated from his personality throughout his long life. Despite his occasional puritanical rants and his later environmental jeremiads, his words convey a joy, a playfulness that is lacking in most adult men, both then and now. "If it were possible to have polymorphic relationships with things, people and the body, would that not be childhood?" Michel Foucault has asked. "This polymorphism is called perversity by the adults, to assure themselves, thus coloring it with the monotonous monochrome of their own sex" (Foucault, *Politics* 117). No wonder Muir was attractive—and remains so to many readers today.

Abounding with desire, the cascades of Muir's most melodic prose take on a new meaning:

> Contemplating the lace-like fabric of streams outspread over the mountains, we are reminded that everything is flowing—going somewhere, animals and so-called lifeless rocks as well as water. Thus the snow flows fast or slow in grand beauty-making glaciers and avalanches; the air in majestic floods carrying minerals, plant leaves, seeds, spores, with streams of music and fragrance; water streams carrying rocks both in solution and in the form of mud particles, sand, pebbles, and boulders. Rocks flow from volcanoes like water from springs, and animals flock together and flow in currents modified by stepping, leaping, gliding, flying, swimming, etc. While the stars go streaming through space pulsed on and on forever like blood globules in Nature's warm heart. (FS 236)

In Muir's ecstatic moments, the word *lavish* is inevitably linked with images of fecundity: "How lavish is Nature building, pulling down, creating, destroying, chasing every material particle from form to form, ever changing, ever beautiful" (FS 238). By the conclusion of his first summer in the Sierra, Muir finds he has been

> constantly reminded of the infinite lavishness of fertility of Nature— inexhaustible abundance amid what seems enormous waste. And yet when we look into any of her operations that lie within reach of our minds, we learn that no particle of her material is wasted or worn out. It is eternally flowing from use to use, beauty to yet higher beauty;

and we soon cease to lament waste and death, and rather rejoice and exult in the imperishable, unspendable wealth of the universe, and faithfully watch and wait the reappearance of everything that melts and fades and dies about us, feeling sure that its next appearance will be better and more beautiful than the last. (FS 242–43)

These are the breaks and flows of desire, the "lovework" of nature itself.

At the end of this emotionally stimulating—and one would have to believe *exhausting*—summer, Muir settled down to a part-time job, sawing fallen timber in Yosemite Valley for James M. Hutchings. But Muir was to have no rest, physically or emotionally. Hutchings was the proprietor of the valley's first hotel; faced with an ever-increasing flow of tourists, he had plans to expand his facilities. At the same time, his land claim in Yosemite Valley was in danger of being revoked by the federal government's efforts to secure the valley as a park; so he needed to make a trip to Washington, D.C., to fight for his claim. Thus, when Muir showed up seeking employment, Hutchings found not only the sawyer he needed, but someone to take care of the hotel and to attend to his family—in particular his wife, Elvira, who has been variously described as "many years younger than her husband . . . a frail, Madonna-like woman with a passionate love of beauty in flowers and art" (Wolfe, *Son of the Wilderness* 126); as "a dreamy, ethereal young woman" (Frederick Turner 204); and as one who "seemed to float rather than walk" (Fox 17). Shortly after hiring Muir in November, Hutchings left the valley for his trip east, not returning until May. For at least some of these long winter months, Muir lived with the Hutchings family—sans old James. The Hutchings's marriage, it is said, was characterized by tension, and this, coupled with the obvious friendship that developed between Muir and Elvira, has been a persistent source of rumor in Yosemite Valley even down to this day.[9] The exact nature of their relationship is unknown, but it has prompted one biographer to write: "Something did happen, though precisely what can only be conjectured" (Fox 17). Whatever might have "happened" between the two, we can be assured that there was an emotional intensity on Muir's

---

9. Elvira, some years later, did leave her husband and marry another man.

part. Nor should his unquestionable love of children be over-
looked: Elvira Hutchings had three and Muir was particularly fond
of them, as they were of him. If we keep in mind the exhilarating
summer he had just passed in the high country, we find in Linnie
Marsh Wolfe's reserved depiction of this new phase in Muir's life a
certain erotic suggestion: "John had come into the Yosemite ex-
pecting to pass a solitary winter. He was therefore surprised to find
here in the heart of the mountains so charming a group as the
Hutchings family" (Wolfe 126). If nothing else, Muir did escape
his loneliness, at least for the time being.

Despite the tension that prevailed between him and his father,
Muir remained deeply attached emotionally to his own family (especially to his mother and his sister Sarah) and he never divested
himself—even during his pilgrim years—of the domestic urge. Desire, for many people, can be securely impounded in the family,
and Muir was such a person. To his sister Sarah, he would write:
"Little did I think when I used to be, and am now, fonder of home
and still domestic life than any of the boys, that I only should be a
bachelor, and doomed to roam always outside the family circle"
(qtd. in Wolfe, *Son of the Wilderness* 199). The issue is not whether
Muir and Elvira ever had sexual relations, but that they were *emotionally* intimate—with him playing the role of surrogate father to
her children, which perhaps allowed him to become the kind, af-
fectionate father he had dreamed of having himself. Although
Muir's relationship with Elvira Hutchings was yet another expression of desire in his life, it cannot be pinned down and displayed.
When we permit mystery, uncertainty, and doubt to linger in our
appraisal of Muir's life, we sustain a resonance otherwise lost.

A similar suggestiveness resonates in his "involvement" during
the summer of 1870 with the English novelist Thérèse Yelverton.
Most of the speculation about this relationship stems from the fact
that Yelverton made Muir into the hero of her novel *Zanita: A Tale
of the Yo-Semite*. Frederick Turner writes: "Her idealized portrait of
Muir in *Zanita* strongly suggests she had developed more than a literary interest in him" (206). The gossip about Muir's love life does
not stop here. Because some of his letters to Jeanne Carr "are now
missing and others have been crudely mutilated" (381), there has
been no lack of speculators insisting that Muir had some sort of ro-

mantic liaison with her as well.[10] If nothing else, these rumors suggest that Muir at least was not spending *all* of his time at work in the sawmill or in the solitary pursuit of his nature studies. Surprisingly, amid all the unsubstantiated fantasizing about Muir's romantic involvements, little attention has been focused on the tangible evidence of his love-making to the world: his earliest published writings, those that appeared in the 1870s. These I have chosen to call his "parables of desire."

### The Parables of Desire

Whatever the exact nature of the events that transpired between Muir and the various women in his life, these episodes served over the next two years to heighten his passion and aesthetic response to cascades, torrents, floods, and flows of any sort: the stormier the better. "Nature is a flood and we are all in it," reads one undated fragment in the Muir Papers (qtd. in Engberg and Wesling 107). In a notebook entry, probably written in the summer of 1871, he realizes: "I will follow my instincts, be myself for good or ill, and see what will be the upshot. As long as I live, I'll hear waterfalls and birds and winds sing. I'll interpret the rocks, learn the language of flood, storm and the avalanche" (qtd. in Wolfe 144). This was also the period in which he made his public debut as a writer.

The first full essay to be published under John Muir's name appeared in the April 1872 edition of *The Overland Monthly*. Given Muir's trademark conflation of water and desire, the essay's title is revealing: "Yosemite Valley in Flood" (he first called it "Jubilee of Waters"). The essay opens with a rendering of the Merced River as female, and then, risking a Victorian impropriety, the author informs his readers: "I have lived with her for three years, sharing all her life and fortunes, dreaming that I appreciated her; but I never have so much as imagined the sublimity, the majesty of her music, until seeing and listening at every pore I stood in her temple today" (347). The occasion for these words was an immense winter storm that broke over the valley on December 16, 1871. Amid the

---

10. See Frederick Turner's bibliographical note, p. 381.

"torrents of warm rain" that were melting the snow in the upper mountains, the valley walls suddenly erupted in an "outgush" of waters. After tracing the swelling Merced "as far as the Hutchings'" (interesting in and of itself), Muir comes upon "the most glorious congregation of water-falls ever laid bare to mortal eyes" (348). Having been "laid bare," these waterfalls were now "throbbing out their lives in one stupendous song" and "throbbing out rays of beauty warm and palpable as those of the sun." Unable to restrain his use of the word *throbbing*, he employs it yet again in what might demurely be called the climax of his essay:

> The Merced, in some places, overflows its banks, having risen at once from a shallow, prattling, ill-proportioned stream, to a deep, majestic river. The upper Yosemite is in full, gushing, throbbing glory of prime; still louder spring its shafts of song; still deeper grows the intense whiteness of its mingled meteors; fearlessly blow the winds among its dark, shadowy chambers, now softly bearing away the outside sprays, now swaying and bending the whole massive column. So sings Yosemite, with her hundred fellow-falls, to the trembling bushes, and solemn-waving pines, and winds, and clouds, and living, pulsing rocks—one stupendous unit of mountain power—one harmonious storm of mountain love. (349)

Orgy of description is followed by calm: "On the third day the storm ceased. Frost killed the new falls; the clouds are withered and empty; a score of light is drawn across the sky, and our chapter of flood is finished."

Muir's narrative strategy in this essay—a first-person voice that situates itself in the midst of flood or storm—is indicative of his writing throughout these parables: Each is an autobiographical witness to desire. To argue that "Yosemite Valley in Flood" is, at least on one level, but a thinly disguised sexual fantasy is not to violate the limits of interpretation, especially when we compare it to other literary works that employ a similar structure and imagery.[11] There is no doubt that Muir *loved* to write about the flow of Yosemite's streams: "I never can keep my pen perfectly sober when it gets into the bounce and hurrah of cascades," he admits in one letter (LF

---

11. Instructive, in this regard, is the comparison of Muir's essay with Kate Chopin's short story "The Storm."

149). Certainly, the ecstasy and the intoxication he conveys in his writings commingle with the bounce and hurrah all lovers feel in the presence of the beloved.

Once again, I must stress that we should not restrict our interpretation to the merely sexual.[12] I wish to argue for an understanding of Muir's expression of desire in the widest possible sense. There is always a metaphysical component to desire, and to neglect this aspect of Muir's life and writings would be unfortunate indeed. As he explains himself to Jeanne Carr: "How little do we know of ourselves, of our profoundest attractions and repulsions, of our spiritual affinities! How interesting does man become, considered in his relations to the spirit of this rock and water! How significant does every atom of our world become amid the influences of those beings unseen, spiritual, angelic mountaineers that so throng these pure mansions of crystal foam and purple granite!" (LF 122). Muir, here and elsewhere, echoes Spinoza's parallelism between body and mind. Instructive in this regard is an 1872 journal passage: "*Gain health* from lusty, heroic exercise, from free firm-nerved adventures without anxiety in them, with rhythmic leg motion in runs over boulders requiring quick decision for every step. Fording streams, tingling with flesh brushes as we slide down white slopes thatched with close snow-pressed chaparral, half-swimming or flying or slipping—all these make good counter-irritants. Then enjoy the utter peace and solemnity of the trees and stars. Find many a plant and bird living sequestered in hollows and dells—little chambers in the hills. Feel a mysterious presence in a thousand coy hiding things" (JOM 98). "There are no harsh, hard dividing lines in nature," he writes in his journal on August 21, 1872. "Glaciers blend with snow and the snow blends with the thin invisible breath of the sky. So there are no stiff, frigid, stony partition walls betwixt us and heaven. . . . Eye hath not seen, nor ear heard, etc., is applicable here, for earth is partly heaven, and heaven earth" (JOM 89).

Despite this apparent resolution of the dualism that has dominated Western thought since Plato, Muir is unable to sustain his

---

12. "In the end one loves one's desire and not what is desired." Nietzsche, *Beyond Good and Evil* 93.

parallelism, as he more often than not falls back on the idealist distinction. "You anticipate all the bends and falls and rapids and cascades of my mountain life," he writes to Jeanne Carr, "and I know
that you say truly about my companions being those who live with
me in the same sky, whether in reach of hand or only of spiritual
contact, which is the most real contact" (LF 131). One wonders
what to make of this philosophical wavering. On one hand, it is
possible to describe Muir as a lesser and late romantic, an epigonic
Transcendentalist; on the other hand, it is equally possible to identify in his writings passages that reflect a sort of emerging Taoism.[13]
This vacillation is most pronounced during the pilgrim years,
when his thoughts on these matters are channeled simultaneously
with his expressions of desire and, as seen in the above letter to
Jeanne Carr, loneliness. To some degree we can say that desire in
Muir's writing is elided in the human and transferred to the non-
human. Some would argue that this is a sublimation in the
Freudian sense; however, given the passionate intensity with
which Muir describes cascades, storms, and indeed the landscape
itself, a more engaging interpretation of his life and work during
this period would underscore his coming to terms with a desire
comparable in magnitude to that of Everett Ruess—vast, wild,
seemingly inexpressible.

Muir, unlike Ruess, succeeded in giving expression to his en-
counters with the wild—through the medium of writing. What
Muir shares with Ruess is the awareness that what he seeks to im-
pound in art resists containment:

> I would fain draw everything in sight—rock, tree, and leaf. But little
> can I do beyond mere outlines,—marks with meanings like words,
> readable only to myself,—yet I sharpen my pencils and work on as if
> others might possibly be benefited. Whether these picture-sheets are
> to vanish like fallen leaves or got to friends like letters, matters not
> much; for little can they tell to those who have not themselves seen
> similar wildness, and like a language have learned it. (FS 131)

After suggesting what amounts here to a wilderness freemasonry,
Muir concludes simply: "It is easier to feel than to realize, or in any

---

13. For a reading of the Taoist elements in Muir's thought, see Cohen.

way explain, Yosemite grandeur." What is most wild escapes signification, but this does not stop the writer from assaying in language the experience of it. This, on the most fundamental level, is what distinguishes Muir from Everett Ruess: Muir was an author and, as such, acknowledged that the source of his art was indeed the wild.

The decision to become a writer was not arrived at easily by John Muir. Perhaps he harbored some of that Puritan suspicion of language, or perhaps he was simply insecure about his own literary abilities. In any case, we find that the year 1872—the middle of his pilgrim wanderings—marks a watershed in Muir's mountain and literary life. It was a momentous year for him, heralded by the Owens Valley earthquake and concluded by his risky winter exploration of Tenaya Canyon; in between, he made his famous first climb of Mt. Ritter and conducted his first cultural forays into San Francisco, city excursions that one commentator has called "the beginning of the end of his heroic mountain solitude" (Frederick Turner 212). In 1872, Muir also settled upon his career as a writer.

In the early morning of March 26, 1872, Muir, inventor of "the early-rising machine," was tossed out of his bed by the "fervid passionate throbbings" of the earth itself. In the context of his biography, this earthquake—one of the most powerful in the historical record of human experience in California—is noteworthy. On one level, it provides a geological analogue to the flows of desire, which, until this point, he had been tasting and tracing only in the living streams and ancient glaciers of the Yosemite Sierra. The entire earth itself, he now discovers, throbs with passion. In a letter to Ralph Waldo Emerson, written in the evening of that same day, Muir recounts his walk, taken despite the many aftershocks. In typical fashion, he asks two violets he finds in Indian Canyon what *they* have to report of the earthquake. Their response: "It's all love" (qtd. in Cohen 134).

The temblor also initiates a tumultuous period in Muir's personal development. At the time of Yosemite's rumblings, Muir was near the end of his thirty-third year, suffering his own rumblings of doubt about the purpose of his life. For more than three years he had been "ploddingly making observations about this valley and the high mountain region to the east of it," observations that led him to conclude that, contrary to the determination of the

renowned geologist Josiah Whitney, the major influence on the
Yosemite landscape was the slow, uniform work of glacial action.
In the previous summer, Muir had discovered the first "living glacier" in the Sierra, garnering him some praise, but as scientists
began to capitalize on his discovery he was becoming increasingly
anxious that the scientific community, while appropriating his
ideas, would not grant him his due. Thus, he was pondering his
first book, the plan for which he lays out in a letter to Jeanne Carr
(LF 104–11).

Ironically, some of Muir's most perceptive writing concerns his
resistance to "book-making" and the inadequacy of language to
convey his own experience. "I have a low opinion of books," he
writes in his journal, "they are but piles of stones set up to show
coming travelers where other minds have been, or at best signal
smokes to call attention" (JOM 94). Jeanne Carr, more than anybody else during this period, encourages Muir to put his "scientific
convictions into crystalline prose for other uses" (qtd. in Cohen
130). Muir, however, resists any suggestion to harden his desire; in
a July response to Carr's most recent urgings, he voices frustration:
"All say *write*, but I don't know how or what." Then, in an apparent reference to the geologists already making use of his ideas, he
says: "I would let others write what I have read here, but they
make so damnable a hash of it and ruin so glorious a unit" (LF
126). By the end of that year, despite signs of his eroding resistance, he is still declaring to her: "Book-making frightens me, because it demands so much artificialness and retrograding" (Badé
ii:6). In this regard, Muir shares ground with his contemporary,
Friedrich Nietzsche, who, when faced with a scholarly book, responds: "We do not belong to those who have ideas only among
books. It is our habit to think outdoors—walking, leaping, climbing, dancing, preferably on lonely mountains or near the sea where
even the trails become thoughtful. Our first questions about the
value of a book, of a human being, or a musical composition: Can
they walk? Even more, can they dance?" (*Gay Science* 322). One
can only gleefully fantasize what these two men would have made
of each other had they met in Yosemite Valley.

Although Muir was inclined toward suspicion of language, his
reluctance to be drawn into "book-making" may equally well be

explained by the fact that the physical process of writing took time away from his joyful peregrinations through the mountains. "Oftentimes when I am free in the wilds I discover some rare beauty in lake or cataract or mountain form, and instantly seek to sketch it with my pencil, but the drawing is always enormously unlike the reality. So also in words . . . [which] make but a skeleton, fleshless, heartless, and when you read, the dead bony words rattle in one's teeth" (LF 146). Nowhere in his published or unpublished writings does he mention the sheer joy of writing, the pleasure that so many other writers attribute to the pen. Unlike Thoreau, Muir never felt the thrill of desire in the cascades of language, but only in actual mountain streams, peaks, and earthquakes; thus, his affinities for singing the wild hover closer to a bird, the water ouzel, than to any literary precursor.[14] For Muir, writing was always work, never release; never did it consummate his desire.

It is not surprising then to find that the most fluid of all Muir's parables of desire is not a "fleshless" article, but a personal letter to Jeanne Carr, a letter Muir never intended for publication. "A Geologist's Winter Walk" begins, uncharacteristically, *in medias res*, with Muir speeding "afoot over the stubble-fields" away from Oakland (after a brief visit) and back toward his Yosemite haven, which he describes in language usually reserved for reunion with the beloved. Keeping in mind his earlier depiction of the Merced as feminine, consider now this portrayal of the mountain Half Dome (a.k.a. Tissiack):

> I was absorbed in the great Tissiack—her crown a mile away in the hushed azure; her purple drapery flowing in soft and graceful folds low as my feet, embroidered gloriously around with deep, shadowy forest. I have gazed on Tissiack a thousand times—in days of solemn storms, and when her form shone divine with jewels of winter, or was veiled in living clouds; I have heard her voice of winds, or snowy, tuneful

---

14. He writes of the water ouzel: "Tracing on strong wind every curve of the most precipitous torrent, from one extremity of the California Alps to the other; not fearing to follow them through their darkest gorges, and coldest snow-tunnels; acquainted with every water-fall, echoing their divine music; and throughout the whole of their beautiful lives interpreting all that we in our unbelief call terrible in the utterances of torrents, as only varied expressions of God's eternal love." See "The Humming-Bird of the California Water-Falls" (554).

waters; yet never did her soul reveal itself more impressively than now. I hung about her skirts, lingering timidly, till the glaciers compelled me to push up the canyons. (355)

In the middle of this letter, he inserts a curious notebook entry specifically addressed to "you," but the pronoun reference is elusive.

Readers of *The Overland Monthly* were informed in an accompanying editorial note that these "letter-pages" were originally sent to a "friend with whom Mr. Muir shares his mountain studies." This alone is insufficient to explain the erotic valence of the language he uses to describe landscape features such as South Dome, "high in the stars, her face turned from the moon, with the rest of her body gloriously muffled in waved folds of granite." And certainly, some eyebrows must have been raised when he concluded this "note-book" entry with what amounts to a goodnight kiss in words for his reader: "How wholly infused with God is this one big word of love that we call the world! Goodnight. Do you see the fire-glow on my ice-smooth slab, and on my two ferns? And do you hear how sweet a sleep-song the fall and cascades are singing?" Although he was preoccupied during this period with fashioning a public persona, an appropriate authorial self both detached and "objective" to convey his scientific ideas, his private self—as expressed in these words to Jeanne Carr—is in deep and recurrent personal confrontation with desire, permeating all of his writing in the pilgrim years, though it is often masked. Here is the fundamental tension in his art.

The essential story of "A Geologist's Winter Walk" is one of pilgrimage. Muir is recounting yet another of his "escapes" from the sordid city, followed by a "rebirth" in the wilderness. After a cleansing baptism in the "bright river" of Yosemite Valley, he informs his reader: "I still felt muddy, and weary, and tainted with the sticky sky of your streets; I determined, therefore, to run out to the higher temples" (355). This urge to liminality, characteristic of all pilgrims, carried him up Tenaya Canyon, which, both then and now, is one of the most inaccessible gorges in the Sierra Nevada. As he scrambled up boulders and sheer granite walls, literally and figuratively tracing his desire along the cascades of Tenaya Creek, Muir "suddenly stumbled, for the first time since I touched foot to

Sierra rocks." The fall he took—call it a "swoon"—was substantial.
"After several involuntary somersaults, I became insensible, and
when consciousness returned, I found myself wedged among short,
stiff bushes, not injured in the slightest. Judging by the sun, I could
not have been insensible very long; probably not a minute, possibly an hour; and I could not remember what made me fall, or
where I had fallen from: but I saw that if I had rolled a little further, my mountain-climbing would have been finished." The accident and its resultant unconsciousness, the involuntary unselfing
of the self, parallel Muir's geographical retreat from society. The
fact that this narrative was intended as a personal letter is fortuitous: the prose retains the unpasteurized spontaneity and trace of
its author, a trace often willfully obscured in much of his published
writings. The narrative concludes on a note of epiphany, the pilgrim's return home in a transformed state of being:

> I ran home in the moonlight, with long firm strides; for the sun-love
> made me strong. Down through the junipers—down through the firs;
> now in shadows, now in white light; over sandy moraines and bare,
> clanking rock; past the huge ghost of South Dome, rising weird
> through the firs—past glorious Nevada—past the groves of Illilou-
> ette—through the pines of the valley; frost-crystals flashing all the sky
> beneath, as star-crystals on all the sky above. All of this big moun-
> tain-bread for one day! One of the rich, ripe days that enlarge one's
> life—so much of sun upon one side of it, so much of moon on the
> other. (358)

For sheer, unmitigated rapture in the presence of the wild, this passage is unrivaled, even by Muir himself in his other writings.

Also of interest in this singular essay from the Muir canon is
yet another expression of his reluctance to adopt a public voice for
his writings. Occurring in the antepenultimate paragraph, it re-
sounds with the unshakable suspicion of book-making that had become, by this point, de rigueur for him: "Now your finger is raised
admonishingly, and you say, 'This letter-writing will not do.'
Therefore, I will not try to register my homeward ramblings. . . . I
will cast away my letter pen, and begin 'Articles,' rigid as granite
and slow as glaciers." His desire, it would seem, was at last beginning to lithify; there is a hint that the wildest of his pilgrim years
were drawing to a close. Although he would spend most of 1873 in

the Sierra, more and more of his time was being devoted to making his "Articles," which appeared with increasing frequency in the periodicals, especially in *The Overland Monthly*. By November, he moved to Oakland, with the express purpose to write his "book" on the glacial geology of the Sierra.[15] Here he remained until the following August, beginning his literary career in earnest, fulfilling a prophecy he penned in his journal the year before: "Well, perhaps I may yet become a proper cultivated plant, cease my wild wanderings, and form a so-called pillar or something in society, but if so, I must, like a revived Methodist, learn to love what I hate and to hate what I most intensely and devoutly love" (JOM 93).

### Auld Lang Syne

In September 1874, having completed his working sojourn in the city, Muir returned to the mountains. Back at his Yosemite "home" after a ten-month absence, he writes to Jeanne Carr: "On leaving Oakland I was so excited over my escape that, of course, I forgot and left all the accounts I was to collect. No wonder, and no matter. I'm beneath that grand old pine that I have heard so often in storms both at night and in the day. It sings grandly now, every needle sun-thrilled and shining and responding tunefully to the azure wind."[16] A companion piece to "A Geologist's Winter Walk," this letter serves as a kind of anti-strophe: It too renders a story of pilgrimage, the *same* pilgrimage, along the same path (though now including a train ride) to Yosemite, more or less employing the same narrative strategy he used in that missive so unexpectedly published in *The Overland Monthly*.

Consistent with the paradigm of pilgrimage laid out by Victor Turner and other anthropologists, Muir's account documents a "trying journey" from the Bay Area to Yosemite Valley that functions as an ascetic purification. After detraining in Turlock, he at

---

15. This work, accomplished in Oakland, eventually appeared as a series of seven articles in *The Overland Monthly* between 1874 and 1875. The seven essays were not brought together and published as a single volume until 1949, thirty-five years after Muir's death. See William Colby, ed., *John Muir's Studies in the Sierra*.

16. Subsequent citations drawn from Badé ii:10–27.

last begins to walk. "The freedom I felt was exhilarating, and the burning heat and thirst and faintness could not make it less. Before I had walked ten miles I was wearied and footsore, but it was real earnest work and I liked it. Any kind of simple natural destruction is preferable to the numb, dumb, apathetic deaths of a town." He then exclaims: "I was wild once more and let my watch warn and point as it pleased." He has crossed a threshold, able again to read "lessons" in the landscape, this time in the form of a lizard's trace in the sand: "I knew that mountain boulders moved in music; so also do lizards, and their written music, printed by their feet, moved so swiftly as to be invisible, covers the hot sands with beauty wherever they go." Although Muir "glowed with wild joy" in this discovery, the overall import of this narrative, unlike the epiphany he achieves in "A Geologist's Winter Walk," seems directed more toward expounding a simple escape (or its failure) than any form of spiritual enlightenment. Instead, we find him striding away "with my own feet sinking with a dull craunch, craunch, craunch in the hot gray sand, glad to believe that the dark and cloudy vicissitudes of the Oakland period had not dimmed my vision in the least."

Nevertheless, the "Oakland period" appears to have affected his aesthetic vision, as the latter part of this narrative is haunted by a vague melancholy. When he finally reaches the Merced River at the Central Valley town of Hopeton, he finds the townspeople "all were yellow and woebegone with malarious fever." He follows the river, slowly making his way toward Yosemite. Despite his efforts to render the beauty of the "wild river," he is unable to shake his gloominess. Indeed, on a plateau of sugar pines, in the midst of a reunion with his old friend A. G. Black, the stillness of the early evening is suddenly shattered by a dismal wailing:

> About eight o'clock a strange mass of tones came surging and waving through the pines. "That's the death song," said Black, as he reined up his horse to listen. "Some Indian is dead." Soon two glaring watch-fires shone red through the forest, marking the place of congregation. The fire glare and the wild wailing came with indescribable impressiveness through the still dark woods. I listened eagerly as the weird curves of woe swelled and cadenced, now rising steep like glacial precipices, now swooping low in polished slopes. Falling boulders and

rushing streams and wind tones caught from rock and tree were in it. As we at length rode away and the heaviest notes were lost in distance, I wondered that so much of mountain nature should well out from such a source. Miles away we met Indian groups slipping through the shadows on their way to join the death wail. (Badé ii:21–22)

Free of Muir's usual antipathy for Indians, this passage becomes all the more remarkable. Although it would be inaccurate to say that he is empathizing here with the Miwoks, he seems for once to recognize the Indians' affinity with the natural world, an affinity that, had he taken more interest in them, he might have recognized as akin to his own.

The "death-song" episode highlights the valedictory quality of the entire letter. Although he painstakingly attempts to write a narrative of reunion, he inevitably lapses into farewell. "Few nights in my mountain life have been more eventful than that of my ride in the woods from Coulterville, where I made my reunion with the winds and pines. It was eleven o'clock when we reached Black's ranch. I was weary and soon died in sleep." The next day, when he arrives in Yosemite Valley, he finds: "No one of the rocks seems to call me now, nor any of the distant mountains. Surely this Merced and Tuolumne chapter of my life is done." One can sense in these words the tone of an abandoned lover; understandably, readers have speculated from them about the nature of Muir's relationship to Jeanne Carr. "I have been out on the river bank with your letters," he tells her. "How good and wise they seem to be! You wrote better than you knew. Altogether they form a precious volume whose sentences are more intimately connected with my mountain work than any one will ever be able to appreciate." Muir took her letters to read beside the Merced River, so often the erotic drainage in his own writings. It is fruitless, however, to attempt any critical reduction here and separate the strands of Muir's desire: His words are directed as much to Yosemite, to the wild itself, as they are to Jeanne Carr. "I will not try [to] tell the Valley. Yet I feel that I am a stranger here. I have been gathering you a handful of leaves." A handful of leaves to add to the sheaf he has just finished composing in Oakland. "Remember me to my friends," he concludes on a doleful note, his goodnight kiss delivered with the miserable awkwardness of a former lover. "I trust you are not now so overladen. Good-night. Keep the goldenrod and yarrow. They are auld lang syne."

Although the "Merced and Tuolumne chapter" of his life was over, the most intense chapter of his experience with the wild was just beginning. The next four months would be dominated by mountain storms, converging at the aesthetic and psychological core of Muir's oeuvre. He once expressed displeasure for the word *storm*, which he insisted was "a most damnable name for the flowering of the clouds" (Badé i:367). He never tired of referring to snow as "flowers." Like the Sierra streams and cascades, storms for Muir were always charged with erotic potential. During this important segment of his life, a time that found him holding down a respectable job (of sorts) and holding off a swelling loneliness, storms became the unmistakable locus of desire.[17]

### The Lost Sierra

Following the valedictory letter he sent to Jeanne Carr, Muir wasted no time in making his way into the high mountains, eventually crossing the Sierra crest to explore the eastern slope of the range from Mono Lake north to Tahoe. He recovered something of his former mountain self, as we can see in what one biographer has called "a most significant letter" (Wolfe, *Son of the Wilderness* 176) to Jeanne Carr: "I was alone, and during the whole excursion, or period rather, was in a kind of calm, uncurable ecstasy. I am hopelessly and forever a mountaineer" (LF 168). In the context of his recent melancholy and the extensive wanderings he was now engaged in, Muir's words, in this letter, seem less than earnest. For the next two and a half years, his mood would be characterized less by "uncurable ecstasy" than by agitated loneliness. Loneliness, a by-product of desire, perhaps results from the recognition of the vastness of erotic space, a void wherein the self seems "nothing."

---

17. For the next several years, in fact, Muir was a regular contributor to the San Francisco *Daily Evening Bulletin*. Thus, he was able to finance his wanderings by writing about them; he had become a professional writer.

By the end of October, Muir had arrived at Sisson's, near Mount Shasta, and on November 2 he reached the mountain's summit. In his account of the ascent of this 14,161-foot volcano, rather than boast of the solitary mountaineering exploits that brought him to such a formidable height, he is preoccupied with describing the storms that roll in upon the peak. The storms of that particular autumn had been falling "with special emphasis upon the lofty cone of Shasta, weaving and felting its lavish cross of snow-crystals, fold over fold, and clothing the whole massive mountain in richest winter white" (Engberg 30). Muir, once again wielding the word *lavish*, finds himself caught in one of these storms, which kindles in him a passion cognate with the one he had known in the presence of Yosemite streams: "All kinds of clouds began to fuse into one, the wind swept past in hissing floods, and the storm closed down on all things, producing a wild exhilaration" (36). This would be the first in a series of four storms over the next six months that Muir would render into prose.

Following the Shasta excursion, he made his way southward along the west slope of the Sierra to Knoxville (today known as Brownsville), where he paid a two-month visit to his old sweetheart, Emily Pelton, who was now living there with relatives. It was a creative time in Muir's life, spawning one of his most famous mountaineering narratives, but it is also a period of dithering desire, his aesthetic interest shifting between cascades and "dead rivers" and storms, as the channel of his personal intimacies decidedly swings away from Jeanne Carr, momentarily flowing again in and around Emily Pelton before discharging into the vastness of the Great Central Valley, resolving at last in the calm tangle of the Sacramento Delta and Suisun Bay, where he encounters the woman who would become his wife. These Knoxville days suffuse Muir's parables of desire with rippling climax.

The area that was Knoxville has not changed significantly since Muir's day, save that the forest is now denser, having recovered from the unregulated harvesting of timber and innumerable wildfires that occurred in the nineteenth century. Here, the land folds itself into significant hills, that segment of the western Sierra slope which modulates between foothill and true mountain, elevations between valley and ridge crest running from two to three thousand feet. The region is remote from large urban centers, so it remains sparsely populated and is said to sport good fishing. The local chamber of commerce wistfully refers to their environs as "The Lost Sierra." If you go to Brownsville and inquire about John Muir's visit there from December to January 1874–75, you will be hard-pressed to uncover information: a few people will have heard of him, but they will know little about his visit to Knoxville; fewer still will know that Brownsville, in fact, was once called Knoxville; and nobody will have heard of Emily Pelton. Whatever record might have existed of the actual relationship between Muir and Emily Pelton during these two months, it—like this portion of the Sierra—seems to have been lost.

Between 1864 and 1872, Muir had fallen out of contact with Pelton, the woman whom he "had almost certainly once considered marrying" (Engberg 65), but now they had resumed correspondence. In recommencing with her, he hints at the barely suppressed loneliness that characterized his pilgrim years: "In all these years since I saw you I have been isolated; somehow I don't mould in with the rest of mankind and have become far more confusedly bashful than when I lived in the Mondell [House]" (Badé i:321). Emily must have recognized at once that Muir had not changed much since the last letter she had received from him, one that he composed hastily in a train station on March 1, 1864: "I am to take the cars in about half an hour. I really do not know where I shall halt. I feel like Milton's Adam and Eve—'The world was all before them where to choose their place of rest'" (116). Though haunted by loneliness, he still harbored that insatiable wanderlust.

I wonder about the tenor of their relationship in California. "Dear Friend Emily," Muir writes from Yosemite in 1872 to express his desire that she should visit him there: "I would like to have a week of naked, unoccupied time to spend with you" (Badé i:324). Perhaps remembering an old reluctance on her part, he goes on to adopt that old self-righteousness for which he was known at the Mondell House: "People who come here ought to abandon and forget all that is called business and duty, etc.; they should forget their individual existences, should forget they are born. . . . It is blessed to lean fully and trustingly on Nature, to experience, by taking to her a pure heart and unartificial mind, the infinite ten-

derness and power of her love." These are the words of a man confused by desire. Perhaps all he really needed from Emily was a walk
together, a touch of hands, a kiss. He makes his case for "Nature,"
for the "power of her love," too stridently, especially to a woman
who already is too familiar with *his* style of love. After all, he was
the one who *walked away* from her before.

Muir's capacity for "tenderness" has undergone too much of a
displacement from human beings; and when Emily warns him
about this, he responds: "You mention the refining influences of
society. Compared with the intense purity and cordiality and
beauty of Nature, the most delicate refinements and cultures of
civilization are gross barbarisms." He apparently forgets that "cordiality" is itself a "most delicate refinement" of civilization. Muir,
at this stage, also implicitly excludes from his notion of refinement
any form of intense lovemaking between human beings; certainly,
he never wrote about a human lover with the passion he reserved
for the natural world. What was Emily to make of all this dissonance? In a particularly shrill passage in the letter, he writes: "As
for the rough vertical animals called men, who occur in and on
these mountains like sticks of condensed filth, I am not in *contact*
with them; I do not live with them. I live alone, or, rather, with
rocks and flowers and snows and blessed storms; I live in blessed
mountain *light*, and love nothing less pure." It is difficult to deny
the misanthropy here, and the interpretation of these words is
complicated by the fact that they are addressed to his former
"lover." Perhaps Muir's love of storms was all a reflection of his
own storm of emotions, apparently ongoing until the end of his
pilgrim years, when he finally established his own family.

In recent years, passages such as this from his letter to Emily
Pelton have been interpreted as examples of Muir's "non-anthropocentric worldview," a perspective that has come to be known
popularly as "deep ecology."[18] Whereas many passages in Muir's
prose lend support to this sort of reading, ultimately such practice
is to ignore—and, indeed, to deny—the complex torrents of desire
that surged through his personality. Proponents of a philosophy of

---

18. See Tobias; Sessions and Devall.

deep ecology (using the word *philosophy* quite loosely), in their normative eagerness, inevitably overlook the fact that most of us—including John Muir—have *deep* psychological tensions (one might say "problems") that color everything we do, make, say, express. Thus, when we read John Muir, we at least need to pose the question: How much of his "love" for nature resulted from his inability to express love—in its fullest sense—to another human being? Indeed, Muir did have a tremendous capacity to love; this is clear, but in some very important channels of his personality the flow was impeded. In this sense, he was at odds with himself. On one hand, he had no love for the "condensed sticks of filth" (that is, the tourists, hotel workers, and other residents of Yosemite—not to mention all the inhabitants of San Francisco and Oakland), but on the other hand, in any individual encounter with a fellow human being he always displayed great generosity. He showed tremendous affection for children and for his close friends; nevertheless, misanthropy is persistent in his writings.

There is an obvious, and quite ironic, contradiction in his position: Muir was a man who insisted that "everything's hitched to everything else," but he had great difficulty in hitching himself to his own species. Although he condemned those who would "draw sharp dividing lines in nature," he himself draws the sharpest lines of all—between humans and nature. Everything *is* connected to everything else, humans not excluded, and desire, especially for humans, is often what does the connecting. John Muir "loves" nature—but he is also a product of that same nature, and as such is himself, together with all those "sticks of condensed filth," part and parcel of nature. Humans are just another thread in the woof and warp of the ecological tapestry. Although an attitude such as this comes closer to the "non-anthropocentric," we cannot say with any conviction that this is Muir's attitude in the end. For him, the dividing lines are always there, establishing a tension between the particular and the general that is never resolved—it charges all of his writings, and perhaps, too, all of his walking.

In any case, an interpretation of Muir's writings based solely on the assumption that his worldview was "non-anthropocentric" is simply inadequate. The "deep-ecology" perspective offers little to explain Muir's psychological motivations, as when he writes to Emily: "Your broad pages are received. You must never waste letter time in apologies for size. The more vast and prairie-like the better." To take these words beyond a picturesque figure of speech, I would argue that Muir is here acknowledging that what separates him from Emily is a vastness which words, no matter how large they may be writ, could never fill—the vast space that always separates the lover from the beloved. His could never be an "indoor" love. Whatever affection existed between them found its greatest expression in the long walks they took together, first along the slow Wisconsin River, then along the meadowy Merced, and finally along the rocky banks of Dry Creek in Yuba County.

Muir did have an ostensible reason for his extended stay in Knoxville during the winter of 1874–1875: to continue his studies of Sierran geology. He spent lengthy days exploring the ancient riverbeds of the Yuba drainage, the same riverbeds that contain the gold-bearing gravels, which until just before Muir's visit had been subject to extensive hydraulic mining that wreaked environmental havoc upon the watershed's ecology. Apart from the scientific interest the ancient riverbeds aroused in him, they also seem to have opened a channel of desire reminiscent of what he felt in the living streams of the Sierra. To Jeanne Carr (addressing her as "My dear Mrs. Mother Carr"), he writes: "*I have seen a dead river*—a sight worth going round the world to see. The dead rivers and dead gravels wherein lies the gold form magnificent problems, and I feel wild and unmanageable with the intense interest they excite" (LF 176). He then adds, "I have been spending a few fine social days with Emily, but now work." These "dead rivers" signify Muir's own rivers of desire, those that once flowed or are still flowing but now receding, toward Jeanne Carr, toward Emily Pelton. This is not to say that desire was abandoning Muir; on the contrary, the storm door was open. "How gloriously its storms!" he writes in conclusion. "The pines are in ecstasy, and I feel it and must go out to them. I must borrow a big coat and mingle in the storm and make some studies. Farewell. Love to all." All of this serves as a useful preface to Muir's most vivid "storm narratives."

In fact, after finishing this letter Muir marched directly into the storm and wrote up the events in an essay that would be his last contribution to *The Overland Monthly*. It bears the title "Flood-Storm in the Sierra," but it can be read easily as a "flood-storm of desire," bearing comparison to his first *Overland* piece, "Yosemite Valley in Flood." Muir, in this latest essay, "vividly" recalls that earlier "wild storm morning in Yosemite, when a hundred water-falls . . . came and sung together" ("Flood-Storm" 490). In the present storm, however, Muir notes that never before had he "beheld water falling from the sky in denser or more passionate streams. . . . The alders and willows were standing waist-deep, bearing up against the current with nervous gestures . . . while supple branches bending over the flood dipped lightly and rose again as if stroking the wild waters in play." The sugar pines are bemingled with ardor, "bowing solemnly and tossing their giant arms as if interpreting the very words of the storm while accepting its wildest onsets with a passionate exhilaration." Even the miners' materialist desires for gold are subsumed by the grand flow of the creek, "now a booming river as large as the Tuolumne, its current brown with mining-mud washed down from many a 'claim,' and mottled with sluice-boxes, fence rails, and many a ponderous log that had long lain above its reach." The desire Muir perceives inundates all, an irresistible destructive–creative force. The storm (a "flowering of clouds") is an exuberant revelation of fertility: "when I looked down among the budding hazels, and still lower to the young violets and fern-tufts on the rocks, I noticed the same divine methods of giving and taking, and the same exquisite adaptations of what seems an outbreak of violent and uncontrollable force to the purposes of beautiful and delicate life." Toward the end of this narrative, he finds "[y]oung violets, smilax, fruitillaria, saxifrage, were pushing up through the streaming ground as if conscious of all their coming glory; and innumerable green and yellow buds, scarce visible before the storm, were smiling everywhere, making the whole ground throb and tingle with glad life" (494). The "giving and taking," the "throb and tingle" of which he speaks are the gifts and piracies of desire. Heraclitus has joined Muir on this hike.

The most famous of Muir's storm narratives recounts a gusty disturbance that occurred in December; he called it "A Wind Storm in the Forests of the Yuba." Chronologically, the events in this essay precede those of "The Flood-Storm," but the actual composition occurred some time later; the essay itself did not appear until 1878. It opens: "The mountain winds, like the dew and rain, sunshine and snow, are measured and bestowed with wise love upon the forests, with reference to the development of their highest beauty and well-being" ("Wind Storm" 55). The wind, "now whispering and cooing . . . now roaring like the ocean," is imbued with an "ineffable beauty." On this particular Knoxville day, the sky was breathgivingly clear, as it so often is in Northern California after a winter rain. When the wind "began to sound," Muir "lost no time in pushing out into the woods to enjoy it" amid gusts so strong trees were "heard falling for hours at the rate of one every two or three minutes." In the thick of this aeolian upheaval, the "Douglas spruces, with long sprays drawn out in level tresses, and needles massed in a gray, shimmering glow, presented a most striking appearance," and the madrones reflected sunshine "in throbbing spangles" (57). Muir "drifted on through the midst of this passionate music and motion" in a "tingling scramble," until, arriving at the summit of the highest ridge in the neighborhood, it occurred to him "that it would be a fine thing to climb one of the trees to obtain a wider outlook." He chose a Douglas spruce (commonly known today as Douglas fir) in the midst of a group whose "lithe, brushy tops were rocking and swirling in wild ecstasy." Muir quickly mounted the hundred-foot tree, where, at the top, "never before did I enjoy so noble an exhilaration of motion. The slender tops fairly flapped and swished in the passionate torrent, bending and swirling backward and forward, round and round, tracing indescribable combinations of vertical and horizontal curves, while I clung with muscles firm braced, like a bobolink on a reed" (57)— or like a lover to the body of the beloved.

The essay achieves its climax in the same language Muir always so fondly used to render his cascade ecstasies: "The sounds of the storm corresponded gloriously with this wild exuberance of light and motion. The profound bass of the naked branches and boles booming like water-falls; the quick, tense vibrations of the pine needles, now rising to a shrill, whistling hiss, now falling to a silky murmur; the rustling of laurel groves in the dells, and the keen metallic click of leaf on leaf" (58). No matter how many times

Muir depicts natural phenomena in this sensual language, one is always impressed with his unbridled passion but, at the same time, puzzled that he never wrote with such verve about a human being. Perhaps his silence in these matters can be attributed to Victorian propriety, but this only serves to make any understanding of the reception of his writings—especially by the environmentalist community—all the more problematic. Muir was incapable of directly confronting desire as it manifested itself between human beings. Thus, he offers us no words, no advice, on the dire social problems plaguing the Bay Area cities in his day; nor does he offer any words, any advice, on individual relationships, especially those between lovers. He does, though, offer his readers an eloquent testimony against the ravenous utilitarianism with which humans consume the world. "We all travel the milky way together, trees and men," he writes, "but it never occurred to me until this storm-day, while swinging in the wind, that trees are travelers, in the ordinary sense" (59). Trees are pilgrims, too, as the pilgrim Muir tells us: "They make many journeys, not very extensive ones, it is true; but our own little comes and goes are only little more than tree-wavings—many of them not so much." Tree-wavings reflect our own undulations of desire, and though Muir never adequately expressed in words his own carnal and communal desires—namely, the pleasures of lovers and of friends—his writings of the natural world are by no means remote from these joys.

We do not know how Muir and Emily Pelton finally resolved their relationship. By the time he returns to Oakland, in February, we find him again recounting, in a letter to his sister, that old loneliness:

> I thought of you all gathered with your little ones enjoying the sweet and simple pleasures that belong to your lives and loves. I have not yet in all my wanderings found a single person so free as myself. Yet I am bound to my studies, and the laws of my own life. At times I feel as if driven with whips, and ridden upon. When in the woods I sit at times for hours watching birds or squirrels or looking down into the faces of flowers without suffering any feeling of haste. Yet I am swept onward in a general current that bears on irresistibly. When, therefore, I shall be allowed to float homeward, I dinna, dinna ken, but I hope. (Badé ii:48)

The last sentence, with its homespun longing, underscores Muir's domestic urge: He wants a family of his own, but for now that desire has to be steered into vicarious channels.

To judge from his published writings, one would think that he wandered through the mountains in a perpetual state of rapture, but his letters and especially his journals from these pilgrim years reveal a profound loneliness. "I expect to be entirely alone in these mountain walks," he once wrote to Jeanne Carr, "and, notwithstanding the glorious portion of daily bread which my soul will receive in these fields where only the footprints of God are seen, the gloamin' will be lonely" (LF 103). Then he adds, perhaps as much to convince himself as to convince her: "but I will cheerfully pay the price of friendship *all* besides." Muir simply lacks conviction in this regard, especially when we encounter journal entries like the one from 1872 designated "Loneliness": "There perhaps are souls that never weary, that go always unhalting and glad, tuneful and songful as mountain water. Not so, weary, hungry me. In all God's mountain mansions, I find no human sympathy, and I hunger" (JOM 89). And if anyone harbors suspicions that Muir was some kind of hermit, there is this entry from March 15, 1873: "To ask me whether I could endure to live without friends is absurd. It is easy enough to live out of material sight of friends, but to live without human love is impossible. Quench love, and what is left of a man's life but the folding of a few jointed bones and square inches of flesh? Who would call that life?" (138).

Muir spent the period from 1875 to 1877 in alternately exploring the American West and transforming his experiences into articles. Toward the end of this time, in August and September of 1877, he paid a visit to the Carrs in their new home in the southern California "colony" of Pasadena. From here Muir explored the San Gabriel Mountains, encapsulating these ramblings in a pair of essays that appeared in the San Francisco *Daily Evening Bulletin*. These pieces are worthy of mention for two reasons. In the first place, Muir offers his views on a social problem; specific social commentary, in and of itself, is rare enough in his writings to excite comment, but even more noteworthy is the fact that the issue that engages his attention is none other than homelessness. "After witnessing the bad effect of homelessness, developed to so destructive an extent in California, it would reassure every lover of his race to see the hearty home-building going on here and the blessed contentment that naturally follows it" (Muir, *Steep Trails* 140). In these words, one can hear Muir's own domestic hankering clearly asserting itself. Having grown tired of his decade-long rootlessness in California, he feels—albeit unconsciously—ready to settle down. "Travel-worn pioneers, who have been tossed about like boulders in flood-time, are thronging hither as a kind of terrestrial heaven, resolved at last to rest." The imagery is salient, agnate with that of the "Flood-Storm" essay, wherein we find Dry Creek raging, its "smothered bumping and rumbling of bowlders . . . shoving or rolling forward against one another." By the time he reaches Pasadena, two and a half years later, sufficiently "travel worn" and storm "tossed," John Muir is "resolved to rest." The rumblings are fading.

Even waterfalls fail to excite his passion now. Admittedly, the cascade in Eaton Canyon is no rival to Yosemite Falls, but Muir's description is quite "tame" by comparison to his other writings on this subject. Nevertheless, a disclosure of Eros does occur: "The cliff back of [the falls] and on both sides is completely covered with thick, furry mosses, and the white fall shines against the green like a silver instrument in a velvet case. Here come the Gabriel lads and lassies to make love and gather ferns and dabble away their hot holidays in the cool pool" (149). Missing are the detailed, passionate descriptions we have come to expect from Muir when he discovers a waterfall; instead, he offers only the merest suggestion of desire—the lovemaking and "hot holidays" of the "lads and lassies." Too much for the lonely Muir to bear, he plunges off into the San Gabriel Mountains and spends the next three days crawling on his hands and knees through snake-infested chaparral. The essay concludes on a curious note: "My bread gave out a day before reaching the settlements, but I felt all the fresher and clearer for the fast" (153). Hunger, both physical and spiritual, would harry him during the remaining months of 1877.

## The Float Home

Muir's wanderings in the autumn of 1877 were tinctured with exasperation. In September, he led a party, including the famous botanists Asa Gray and Sir Joseph Hooker, to Mount Shasta in extreme northern California. Following this, he floated down the Sacramento River in a skiff, embarking from the Bidwell Ranch in Chico and drifting Huck Finn-like downstream to Sacramento. Not yet satiated with his outdoor adventures, he took a train to Visalia and immediately launched an insufficiently supplied exploration of the Middle Fork of the Kings River, where he and a companion "nearly starved in the process" (Wolfe, *Son of the Wilderness* 196). The severity of the hunger was such that he complained about it for months afterward. No sooner did he emerge from the southern Sierra wilderness than he built another boat for himself, this time launching into the Merced near Hopeton, floating down into the San Joaquin and out through the delta into Suisun Bay. The journal in which he recorded these events contains on its flyleaf the following notation: "November 27, 1877. Arrive at Strentzel's." As Linnie Marsh Wolfe phrases it, "This records what was probably Muir's first visit to the Alhambra Valley Ranch and the family of which he later became a member" (JOM 244). Although this was not the first time John Muir had met Louie Strentzel, the woman he would marry in 1880, this visit does signal, according to his biographers, the beginning of their courtship. It also marks the end of his pilgrim years.

Two days later, on Thanksgiving, Muir writes from San Francisco to his sister Sarah: "I am far from friendless here, and on this particular day I might have eaten a score of prodigious thank dinners if I could have been in as many places at the same time, but the more I learn of the world the happier seems to me the life you live in near, unjealous, generous sympathy with one another, for I assure you these are blessings scarce at all recognized in their real divine greatness" (Badé ii:85). If we read these words as adequate index of Muir's state of mind at the time, we find them laden with the same domestic cravings that tinge the San Gabriel Valley essay. Muir was longing for a home; he sensed in the Strentzel family the same "generous sympathy" he saw in his sister's family—except that the Strentzels had a vacancy that Muir himself might occupy, in the form of an unwed daughter on the threshold of spinsterhood. Phrasing it in this way may seem insensitive, but circumstantial evidence has led several commentators on Muir's life to suggest that his marriage to Louie was motivated more by opportunity than by passion.

Muir was no gold digger, eventually proving to be a fine husband and father, but the most convincing argument for why he finally married Louie Strentzel seems to be a combination of pilgrim weariness, a yearning for a home, and—perhaps most significantly—a loneliness he could no longer bear. He writes the Strentzels a most poignant "thank-you" letter for the hospitality they had bestowed upon him at the conclusion of his float trip: "I shall not soon forget the rest I enjoyed in your pure white bed, or the feast on your fruity table. Seldom have I been so deeply weary, and as for hunger [a reference to his Kings Canyon expedition], I've been hungry still in spite of it all, and for aught I see in the signs of the stomach may go hungry on through life and into the grave and beyond" (95). What did the Strentzels make of such an enigmatic missive?

This letter brings to a close Muir's pilgrim years. His biography takes on a very "settled" quality after this and, as is the case with the lives of most professional writers, becomes rather unremarkable. "My life is the poem I would have writ, / But I could not both live and utter it," as Thoreau phrases it. The entire second half of Muir's long life still lay before him—including his many trips to Alaska and his career as a foremost figure in American conservationist history. But the storms of desire had passed, and the weather of his life glided into the placid haze of domestic duty, the management of a large fruit ranch, and the sequestered hours of an older author busily rewriting and revising the written fragments of his younger, fugitive self into the authoritative voice of a respectable man of letters.

# FOUR

# The Subterranean Clarence King

> *"Faith" is a fine is a fine invention*
> *When Gentlemen can see—*
> *But Microscopes are prudent*
> *In an Emergency.*
>
> —*Emily Dickinson*

## On the Edge of Myth-Making

Clarence King's life may be the most enigmatic among my writers of the wild, but at the same time he is the most public figure in the group, having served in highly visible government positions, first as head of the Fortieth Parallel Survey and then as the inaugural director of the United States Geological Survey. Little wonder he produced a comparatively small body of work. Nevertheless, these few works—combined with provocative biographical detail—are enough to suggest their author was reticent about the wildest adventures of his life. Mention of King in the histories of the American West is inevitably attended by wistful speculation over his dissipation. Such speculation is practically de rigueur for western historians, the result of meager concrete evidence, much of it anecdotal, collected by a small band of friends and published as a memorial volume a few years after his death.[1] Stories circulate even yet that King's most personally revealing papers were destroyed by those who wished to protect his good name. Whereas his friends liked to say he "evaded into space," the simple fact is that King was overwhelmed by it—space being but another name for the wild. Although he did not physically vanish in the fashion of Everett Ruess, Clarence King did pull off a vanishing act—of the soul.

King's story begins on the floor of the Owens Valley. He is gazing in rapture at Mount Whitney, the "highest land in America."

---

1. See *Clarence King Memoirs*, ed. James D. Hague. Hague's descendants deposited the King archives in the Henry E. Huntington Library in the 1950s.

Having failed to attain the summit on two previous attempts, in recent days he has finally succeeded. It is September 1873:

> I entered for a moment deeply and intimately into that strange realm where admiration blends with superstition, that condition in which the savage feels within him the greatness of a natural object, and forever after endows it with consciousness and power. For a moment I was back in the Aryan myth days, when they saw afar that snowy peak, and called it Dhavalagiri (white elephant), and invested it with mystic power.
>
> These peculiar moments, rare enough in the life of a scientific man, when one trembles on the edge of myth-making, are of interest, as unfolding the origin and manner of savage beliefs, and as awakening the unperishing germ of primitive manhood which is buried within us all under much culture and science.[2]

Trembling on the edge of mythmaking, on the limen of the wild, King has a glimmering of that consciousness Lévi-Strauss, almost a century later, would call "the savage mind." In King's view, the savage mind is "buried" (a significant word in his vocabulary) beneath the weight of "culture and science." At this point, he has been in the West for a decade, but he is near the end of his mountaineering adventures, or as he phrases it: "the pass which divides youth from manhood is traversed, and the serious service of science must hereafter claim me."[3] He is thirty-one years old.

Though he had originally journeyed beyond the hundredth meridian to explore and map a vast portion of California and the Great Basin, King now faced the *terra incognita* of the human mind. For this he was unprepared—his tools failed him, as we can surmise from the conclusion to his account:

> This was the drift of my revery as I lay basking on the hot sands of Inyo, realizing fully the geological history and hard, materialistic reality of Mount Whitney, its mineral nature, its chemistry; yet archaic impulse even then held me, and the gaunt, gray old Indian who came slowly toward me must have subtly felt my condition, for he crouched beside me and silently fixed his hawk eye upon the peak.

---

2. Clarence King, *Mountaineering in the Sierra Nevada* (1872, New York: W. W. Norton and Company, 1935), p. 305. Unless indicated otherwise, all references correspond to this edition.

3. *Mountaineering in the Sierra Nevada* 4th ed. (1874), x.

At last he drew an arrow, sighted along its straight shaft, bringing the obsidian head to bear on Mount Whitney, and in strange fragments of language told me that the peak was an old, old man who watched this valley and cared for the Indians, but who shook the country with earthquakes to punish whites for injustice toward his tribe.

I looked at his whitened hair and keen, black eye. I watched the spare, bronze face, upon which was written the burden of a hundred dark and gloomy superstitions; and as he trudged away across the sands, I could but feel the liberating power of modern culture which unfetters us from the more iron bands of self-made myths. My mood vanished with the savage, and I saw the great peak only as it really is, a splendid mass of granite, 14,887 feet high, ice-chiselled and storm-tinted, a great monolith left standing amid the ruins of a bygone geological empire. (*Mountaineering* 306)

King would become increasingly preoccupied with the "archaic" in his later years—especially as he discerned it in women and in landscape—but from this passage we can already infer clear signs of the deep ambivalence that courses through his personality. The dualism that vexes him is reminiscent of the sort Freud outlines in his psychoanalytic theory: King's "archaic impulse" corresponds to the Freudian "instincts," the foundation upon which the edifice of culture (including science) is erected through the process of sublimation.[4]

King evidently experiences a high level of anxiety as the Indian brings his arrow to bear—that is, casts the mythic eye—upon the "hard, materialistic reality of Mount Whitney." King's own technical reports, generated for the various surveys, grant no authority to this mode of perception. Although the Indian supposedly speaks in "strange fragments of language," this language may have been more coherent than King's own faltering redundancy (for example, his "realizing" reality). At this moment, in confronting the thusness of the Sierra Nevada, King has come not only to the limits of science, but to the limits of language itself—and what's more, the Indian's story, indeed his *explanation* of earthquakes, raises a moral issue for which nineteenth-century American science had no response, save to exclude it from consideration. To some degree,

---

4. See Freud's *Civilization and its Discontents*.

King was sensitive to the plight of native cultures, but—true to his historical moment—he felt no inclination to address the issue, so he immediately proceeds to wax eloquent over "the liberating power of modern culture."

The reader attuned to cultural issues can detect a note of relief in King's tone when the Indian walks away. This departure not only spares the scientist embarrassment, it clears the stage of everything that is nonscientific, permitting Mount Whitney to stand, at last for him, "as it really is." As a scientist and a surveyor, King believes the peak is "really" 14,887 feet high, scientifically determined; nevertheless, he concludes his description of this "real" peak by employing the very unscientific metaphor of "a bygone geological empire." Scientists today say the peak is 14,494 feet, and not only that but, citing tectonic uplift, they assert the mountain is actually getting higher. Rather than "bygone," this range is *up and coming*. Tectonic theory has toppled the old figures of speech; King's "geological empire" does not satisfy the postmodern geologist. Despite this, in his Inyo moment of liminality, he does glimpse the same wild territory in which Thoreau, Muir, Austin, and Ruess all seem so at home. It is a psychological space wherein Clarence King would always remain a stranger.

Charles Olson has written: "I take SPACE to be the central fact to man born in America" (Olson 11). Although one can argue that Olson's use of the word "man" must be understood in a rather restricted sense (that is, as a "white male"), it does apply to Clarence King. Olson's SPACE is nonlocalized, nonverbal. When we try to talk about it, we frame myths, tell stories, proffer theories—but in these various modalities we never capture SPACE itself. Surveying and mapmaking constitute humanity's boldest attempt to inscribe it, cordon it off, name it—yet it still escapes. Of this constant escaping of SPACE, most people remain unaware, thus untroubled. A few—such as writers of the wild—are not only aware of the slippery nature of reality, they even celebrate it. Clarence King, on the other hand, was deeply disturbed by the fluidity of things: a sad irony finally emerges in this man who, though he was so clearly open to uncertainties, mysteries, and doubts, remained manacled to fact and reason. Though he was one of the great strategists of space, thoroughly cataloguing his portion of the

American West, there is a lingering sense that he never really *knew* this place.

The story of Clarence King I wish to tell is one of psychological repression, of a man whose institutional allegiances are in perpetual conflict with his own desires. As Peter Wild describes him: "King was an extremist, not a rebel" (Wild 8). Because an extremist attempts to repress the wild, he pays the higher psychological toll. I will employ Freud's definition of repression, that is, the function within the economy of the psyche of rejecting and keeping something out of consciousness. We need to be alert to the fact that "what is repressed exercises a continuous straining in the direction of consciousness, so that a balance has to be kept by means of a steady counter-pressure," and thus a "constant expenditure of energy . . . is entailed in maintaining a repression" (*General Psychological Theory* 109). It is another manifestation of enantiodromia. King's refusal (or inability?) to dismantle for himself the institutional frameworks of his culture—in particular, the profession of science—precludes the possibility of his expressing the wild in any satisfactory way. Michel Foucault offers a useful comment in this regard: "The term 'institution' is generally applied to every kind of more-or-less constrained, learned behaviour. Everything which functions in a society as a system of constraint and which isn't an utterance, in short, all the field of the non-discursive social, is an institution" (*Power/Knowledge* 197). Though the quality of King's prose falls short of Emerson's or Thoreau's, in many ways his attitude is more representative of what could be called the American attitude toward the wild, one that is deeply ambivalent. King's Indian, with his "hundred dark and gloomy superstitions," is dismissed by King's science—and mainstream American culture.

## A High and Buried Life

Clarence King was born to a merchant family in 1842, in Newport, Rhode Island. His father died in China just six years later, leaving the family in a state of financial insecurity that persisted through King's years of growing up; more than anything else, this may explain his feverish quest in later life to "strike it rich" in the shadowy mines of the West. In 1859, King enrolled in Yale's new Sheffield Scientific School, graduating in 1862 among its first class, under the darkest shadow of the Civil War. Since he came from a pacifist Christian background, the war greatly troubled him; his biographer informs us: "The record is clear that as a youth King was deeply devotional in an orthodox way and prone to claim, 'Religion is my life'" (Wilkins 26n). This same fervor would later animate his study of geology; so it could be said of King that he was always a "true believer," one who needs to pledge allegiance to some form of doctrine, whether it be theology or geology or Eldorado.

Upon graduation, rather than heading for the battlefield, he departed for New York, where he spent a year, as we now say, "trying to find himself." His adventures included fraternizing with a group of aesthetes who styled themselves as the American Pre-Raphaelites, the "practical Ruskinites of the city," as his lifelong friend James Gardiner phrases it (Wilkins 42). Late in 1862, King made a trip to Harvard to attend lectures on glaciology by the famous Swiss geologist Louis Agassiz. "King returned from Cambridge more sure than ever that his vocation lay in geology; in that field, his religious, esthetic, and intellectual interests all converged, and he approached the study of the earth as a quest for ethical and esthetic values fully as much for scientific fact" (42). In 1863, under the influence of the tales he had been hearing about the scientific exploits of Josiah Whitney's California Geological Survey, he headed west with Gardiner.

As luck would have it, they encountered William Brewer, a geologist with the California survey, and King managed to have himself taken on as a volunteer. For the next three years he participated in the pioneering effort to map the Sierra Nevada, the range which these scientists would determine contained the nation's highest mountain. In his own words, supplied to James D. Hague for a biographical notice sometime in the early 1880s, King described with trademark braggadocio the years from 1863 to 1866: "His geological life in California was wholly confined to the Sierra Nevada, and he played a prominent part, first under the leadership of Prof. Wm. H. Brewer, and afterwards as his successor in charge of a party, in a difficult and dangerous exploration of the lofty snow covered range. The same elasticity and endurance which had won him the stroke oar at Yale, made him the most active mountaineer in the survey" (King Papers, HEH A-1). King himself named many of the Sierran peaks and landmarks.

By the beginning of 1867, the ambitious young geologist was back in Washington, D.C., lobbying Congress for the funding of a survey along the fortieth parallel, from the Sierra Nevada to the plains of Wyoming—a corridor one hundred miles wide by a thousand miles long, more or less following the route of the new transcontinental railroad. King not only secured funding, but was appointed director of the survey—quite an achievement for a twenty-five-year-old. Fieldwork for the Fortieth Parallel Survey occupied him and his contingent of scientists, surveyors, and artists for the next six years, with the results published volume by volume beginning in 1870 and culminating in 1878 with King's own massive contribution, *Systematic Geology*. In addition, he found time during these years to write his belletristic *Mountaineering in the Sierra Nevada*, which first appeared in 1871 as a series of essays in the *Atlantic Monthly*; it is for this volume that he is remembered. The other important event in this period of King's biography is his engagement to a woman named "Deany" in Virginia City in 1868, which he broke off shortly thereafter.

The capstone to King's career as a scientist and administrator came in 1879, when he was appointed director of the new United States Geological Survey; much to everyone's surprise, he quit this post less than two years later. At this point, his life becomes more and more puzzling. His own words are as good as any in attempting to explain his departure from the U.S.G.S.: "King's resignation from so important a position was due primarily to his unwillingness to devote his life to executive cares, and a determination to pursue certain geological investigations for which the duties of the Directorship left him no time. Since then he has devoted much time to travel and geological investigation, the results of which will appear later" (King Papers, HEH A-1). Very little from these "investigations" was ever published, so it remains doubtful they were ever conducted in earnest.

King was just under forty years old when he resigned his prestigious position, and he may have been experiencing some sort of

midlife crisis, the nature of which we can only surmise. Were he
not so colorful a figure, well placed and admired in the social ranks
of late-nineteenth-century America, this might well be the point
where he disappears into obscurity; indeed, he practically does, but
some important information does survive, such as the fact that he
made a "secret" marriage in 1888 to a woman of color named Ada
Todd, that the bank in El Paso which he helped to found went in-
solvent in the panic of 1893 (the same year he committed himself
for several months to a sanitarium), and that in 1901 he died in
Phoenix. Thus, the story of Clarence King unfolds as a short and
brilliant career followed by twenty years of obscure nomadism, pursuing the chimeras of mining bonanzas only to find none of them
panning out. Wallace Stegner, more alert to the surfaces of the
American West's history than to its subterranean couplings and
uncouplings, concludes: "Clarence King failed for lack of character, persistence, devotion, wholeness" (21). To some extent this
may be true, but Stegner's assessment seems willfully unsympa-
thetic: it passes over the buried life of Clarence King.

He *was* an extremist—a subterranean alpinist. As one friend
wrote in elegy, "Paradox perhaps enjoyed the hegemony of his
mental states. If he can be said ever to have leaned on anything
among the multitude of phenomena that he touched, paradox may
be called his reliance" (Hague 219). Henry Adams, a close friend,
offers the same insight: "Above all he loved a paradox—a thing,
he said, that alone excused thought. No one, in our time, ever
talked paradox so brilliant" (167). What his friends were wont to
call paradox might more appropriately be rendered as ambivalence.
The word *paradox* conveys a certain comfort with the contradictory state of things, the flux of the world, whereas *ambivalence* suggests a discomfiture with the simultaneity of opposing emotions,
such as love and hate, about some person, object, or idea. In
Clarence King's case, his emotional ambivalence is cathected in
the wild; herein lies the problem. The word *cathexis* literally means
a "holding down or fast," suggesting that any concentration of an
individual's emotional energy directed toward nature itself, slippery as it is, will be fraught with difficulty. When to hold on, when
to let go—if these be lessons, Everett Ruess never learned the former and King never learned the latter.

King's ambivalence manifested itself as impercipience embedded in contraries, as we see in the following passage from *Mountaineering's* introductory essay, "The Range," in which he describes the Sierra as

> a mass of strong light, soft, fathomless shadows, and dark regions of forest. However, the three belts upon its front were tolerably clear. Dusky foot-hills rose over the plain with a coppery gold tone, suggesting the line of mining towns planted in its rusty ravines,—a suggestion I was glad to repel, and look higher into that cool, solemn colonnade. Lifted above the bustling industry of the plains and the melodramatic mining theater of the foot-hills, it has a grand, silent life of its own, refreshing to contemplate even from a hundred miles away. (43)

King, in abhorring the commerce of the lowlands and praising the solemn grandeur of the mountains, is blind to the fact that he himself is playing a key role in extending the boundaries of industry into the mountains by mapping them and locating sites of potentially valuable minerals, as well as weaving the peaks into a narrative that was certain to generate a flux of tourism to the "new American Alps."[5] He is attracted by the "grand, silent life" of the High Sierra but, at the same time, cannot abide the silence: He must name it, inscribe it, put it "in its place."

Perhaps the most poignant example of King's ambivalence toward the wild occurs in the surviving stories of his "hunting" exploits. He included in his biographical notes to Hague the following depiction of himself: "I care very little about my reputation as a geologist, but a good deal as being a fellow not easily scared. You might, if you think best, instance one of the bear fights" (King Papers, HEH A-1). It was left to Thurman Wilkins to pick up this thread, opening his *Clarence King: A Biography* with an account of King's 1871 slaying of a grizzly—a narrative that "was to make a favorite campfire story" (3). Such a tale celebrates its hero's courage

---

5. Nevertheless, there is a strong element of parody directed toward tourists in *Mountaineering*. In regard to the early Yosemite visitors, he writes: "Here all who make California books, down to the last and most sentimental specimen who so much as meditates a letter to his or her local paper, dismount and inflate. If those firs could recite half the droll *mots* they have listened to, or if I dared tell half the delicious points I treasure, it would sound altogether too amusing among these dry-enough chapters" (149).

in the face of wild animals, the conflict between "man and nature." Yet this same vanquisher of grizzlies could write in his personal notebook: "You, Clarence King, never dare to look or speak
of nature save with respect and all the admiration you are capable
of" (King Papers, HEH A-2). The public persona he insisted upon
was in direct opposition to the inner man. No wonder he loved
paradox. Examples of this cognitive dissonance—of a mind at odds
with itself—riddle his lifework, reaching one peak (so to speak) in
*Mountaineering*, where a Ruskinian aestheticism perpetually vies
with a draconian scientism for "control" of the Sierra landscape.


### Administering the Physical World

Clarence King's mountain-climbing narratives bring out the
aesthete in him, the American Pre-Raphaelite. Unfortunately for
his professional reputation, the aesthete had the habit of coming
out while he was engaged in geological survey work. *Mountaineering in the Sierra Nevada*, though comprised of fourteen loosely
linked narrative and descriptive essays relating to his years with
the California Geological Survey, recommends itself more as a collection of picturesque idylls whose prose, though never attaining
the power of John Muir, dallies along the same lyrical thresholds.
In 1888, King wrote an intriguing sentence concerning the ancient poet credited with inventing the idyll as a form: "Alexandrian life produced no engendering minds, her one figure is Theocritus, who tuned his voice to soft Doric melody while lying in
the sun on the thymy slopes of Sicily, getting all the inspiration of
his life from man and nature before he became a courtier at the artificial Egyptian capital" ("Artium Magister" 379). This description of the Alexandrian poet invites comparison to King's own life:
a nineteenth-century Theocritus, whose writerly inspiration was
gathered entirely in his youth in the mountains of the West before
he abandoned this wild setting for more "artificial" pursuits in
Washington, D.C., and New York City. "The beauty of Nature,
King liked to say, had always attracted him more than her struc-
tural order, and so at heart he felt more like an artist than an engi-
neer" (Wilkins 326). King's "sensitivity" to beauty struck more

than one member of the California Geological Survey—including his boss, Josiah Whitney—as dilettantish. "But the sharpest cut at the time came from William Gabb the paleontologist, who made no secret of his contempt for a fellow who preferred to sit on a peak and dream all day over snow mountains in the distance instead of hunting fossils in the gold belt" (Wilkins 58). The peer pressure that King endured in order to do "good science" was a microcosm for the utilitarian urge informing national cultural life in the middle of nineteenth-century America. It is worth noting that the Hudson River School, the first "native" art movement in the United States, had evolved in the decades immediately prior to the war; with its romantic representations of untrammelled America, it paralleled the rise of industrialization, perhaps as cultural compensation for the rapidly dwindling wildlands. The sensitive and artistic Clarence King, moving with a phalanx of geologists whose primary research was directed toward uncovering mineral resource, epitomizes the devouring, ambivalent love America has always expressed for the wild.

Keenly perceptive and eloquent, King was certainly the most imaginative member of the various surveys on which he served. His ascents of the various high peaks of the Sierra and the Cascades of northern California, strenuous as they were, would often bring him to a state of physical and psychological liminality. In the *Mountaineering* essay entitled "Shasta Flanks," he writes that at an elevation of fourteen thousand feet "little is left me but bodily appetite and impression of sense. The habit of scientific observation, which in time becomes one of the involuntary processes, goes on as do heart-beat and breathing; a certain general awe overshadows the mind; but on descending again to lowlands, one after another the whole riches of human organization come back with delicious freshness" (269). Climbs like this lead to a shutting down of the normally overactive human mind, pushing the self to the threshold of simple physical perception—the ego is lulled into quiescence.

Such experience could easily serve as the basis for a form of meditative practice, should one choose, and in itself reflects the universal experience of pilgrimage: the journey to a strange far place, the unselfing of the self, and the return home in an enlightened state of being. King himself writes:

I always feel a strange renewal of life when I come down from one of
these climbs; they are with me points of departure more marked and
powerful than I can account for upon any reasonable ground. In spite
of any scientific labor or presence of fatigue, the lifeless region, with
its savage elements of sky, ice and rock, grasps one's nature, and,
whether he will or no, compels it into a stern, strong accord. Then, as
you come again into softer air, and enter the comforting presence of
trees, and feel the grass under your feet, one fetter after another seems
to unbind from your soul, leaving it free, joyous, grateful! (256)

It is tempting to claim that King is describing a state of enlightenment loosely analogous to the goal of Buddhist practice, but a
close look at the words he uses to render this psychological phenomenon shows that the liminal state, situated as it is in a "lifeless
region" and "savage element," actually seems to him a form of im-
prisonment, one that "fetters" his soul. By "soul" King is referring
to the ego and not the larger universal Self; thus, he clearly departs
from any Buddhist experience of liminality. What King and the
Buddhist do share is a dampering of the ego; for the latter this is
the *goal* of a disciplined practice, whereas for the former it is simply
an unnerving, threatening encounter. The Buddhist hopes to return from such an experience in a state of enlightenment, whereas
for King the return is simply relief.

   There are times when he seems to come so close to a perceptual
"breakthrough" of sorts, but he always backs off; as he does in his
encounter with the mythmaking Indian at the foot of Mount
Whitney. In that same essay, as King gazes at the peak, he confesses:

Silence reigns on these icy heights, save when scream of Sierra eagle
or loud crescendo of avalanche interrupts the frozen stillness, or when
in symphonic fulness a storm rolls through vacant cañons with its
stern minor. *It is hard not to invest these great dominating peaks with consciousness,* difficult to realize that, sitting thus for ages in presence of
all nature can work, no inner spirit has kindled, nor throb of granite
heart once responded, no Buddhistic nirvana-life even has brooded in
eternal calm, within these sphinx-like breasts of stone. (304, emphasis added)

King is a most reluctant writer of the wild, continually refusing to
let the workaday world, its prose and its addiction to the ego, drop

away. Ultimately, he places his faith in the Cartesian myth, the subject/object dichotomy. In this sense, his presence in the midst of so many writers who *do* let go is instructive. We should not lose sight of the reason he "held on" so tenaciously—the pressures within his social and cultural milieu "to do good science." Indeed, King himself did love science, did *believe* in science in the same way he believed in a Christian God, and this belief often intersected his belief in art. The historian Michael L. Smith notes: "As Ruskin had foreseen, geology itself was providing a new aesthetic perspective, and perhaps a new kind of faith" (Smith 75). As noted earlier, King was one who needed to believe in *something*.

We must also remember to place the nineteenth-century geological surveys of the American West in the context of a collective will to truth, one that in fact masks a cultural anxiety stemming from so vast an abutment of enigmatic space, imagined to contain uninhabitable deserts, unscalable mountains, untameable animals, and uncivilizable Indians. The various geological surveys were structured on military models of organization and, indeed, were often escorted by battalions of U.S. Army troops. The surveys mapped and named (or *re*-named where Indian names were deemed to be inappropriate) a vast territory from the Rockies to the Sierra Nevada, all in an effort to impose structure on the apparent formlessness of the wild, intermountain West.

King's opening description of the Pacific Slope forests serves as a case in point: "From Walker's Pass to Sitka one may ride through an unbroken forest, and will find its character and aspect vary constantly in strict accordance with the laws of altitude and moisture, each of the several species of coniferous trees taking its position with an almost mathematical precision" (*Mountaineering* 25). More appropriate to a muster of troops than a vegetational community, this description stands in bold contrast to Muir's response to the same forest: "But few indeed, strong and free with eyes undimmed with care, have gone far enough and lived long enough with the trees to gain anything like a loving conception of their grandeur and significance as manifested in the harmonies of their distribution and varying aspects throughout the seasons, as they stand arrayed in their winter garb rejoicing in storms, putting forth their fresh leaves in the spring while steaming with resiny fragrance, re-

ceiving the thunder-showers of summer, or reposing heavy-laden
with ripe cones in the rich sungold of autumn. For knowledge of
this kind one must dwell with the trees and grow with them, without any reference to time in the almanac sense" (*Mountains of California* 139). Muir's words are most likely addressed to scientists
such as those conducting the surveys in "feathery zeros" of calcula-
tion; more importantly, Muir is criticizing the most formidable
weapon in their campaign against SPACE: namely, time itself as
deployed in the practice of history.

The implicit, never-to-be-articulated question that all the surveys endeavored to answer is: How do we control SPACE? On an
individual basis, each of us attempts to establish a relationship to
our space through narrative, telling stories about it, about ourselves within it. This is a form of mythopoeisis practiced by the
Owens Valley Indian who told King that Mount Whitney was an
old man watching over the Native Americans. Stories take place
in time. The science of geology has always been predicated upon
the story of the earth, although this narrative basis is often forgotten after the story is institutionalized as "fact." Near the conclusion of the Fortieth Parallel Survey work in 1877, King would
write: "It is the business of geology to work out the changes of the
past configuration of the globe and its climate; to produce a series
of maps of the successive stages of the continents and ocean
basins, but it is also the business to investigate and fix the rates of
change. Geology is not solely a science of ancient configuration. It
is also a history of the varying rates and mode of action of terrestrial energy." In asserting that geology is not only a history of the
earth but a history of energy, King is staking a grand claim to
power for his science, a power that would supplant all previous
(that is, mythopoetic) powers. Near the beginning of his *Systematic
Geology*, a massive tome whose preponderant size itself wagers
against SPACE, King announces, "this Exploration has actually
covered an epitome of geological history." Fifteen years later, in yet
another interpretive effort to control space through the ordering of
time, King would author an essay that fixed the age of the earth at
twenty-four million years.[6]

---

6. "The Age of the Earth." Scientists today posit the earth's age at about 4.5
*billion* years.

The psychologist Julia Kristeva has pointed out that "the person who does the interpretation, the subject who makes the connection between the sign and the signified, is . . . displaying, on the one hand, the extraordinary architectonics of his will and, on the other, his mastery of time (both momentary and infinite)" (*Kristeva Reader* 305).[7] Providing further amplification of this theme, Lévi-Strauss argues that when a culture sides with history, diachrony prevails over synchrony; thus, history becomes a means of aggressively controlling an otherwise wild space and its enigmatic flux of atemporal elements.[8] Liminality itself is an atemporal experience, and, as such, presents a threat to any institutional power that commits itself to the project of history. Foucault has elaborated on this particular power dynamic:

> A critique could be carried out of this devaluation of space that has prevailed for generations. Did it start with Bergson, or before? Space was treated as the dead, the fixed, the individual, the immobile. Time, on the contrary, was richness, fecundity, life, dialectic. For all those who confuse history with the old schemas of evolution, living continuity, organic development, the progress of consciousness or the project of existence, the use of spatial terms seems to have an air of anti-history. If one started to talk in terms of space that meant one was hostile to time.[9]

King frequently gazed into space of a kind no government survey can enter. Such space is not "hostile" to time—it simply has nothing to do with it. The world in a grain of sand. Pilgrims journeying through this space leave no trace. This is no country for

---

7. Kristeva's words apply equally to her own writing—as they do to mine. This vortex has its origins in language itself but quickly extends into all our endeavors. It is the affliction of positivism to be blind to this fact, the chronic effects of which can be witnessed in the sad practice of all the so-called "resource management" agencies within the federal government.

8. See *The Savage Mind.*

9. "Questions on Geography," in *Power/Knowledge* (70). In another interview in the same collection, Foucault further elaborates: "A whole history remains to be written of *spaces*—which would at the same time be the history of *powers* (both these terms in the plural)—from the great strategies of geo-politics to to the little tactics of habitat, institutional architecture from the classroom to the design of hospitals, passing via economic and political installations. . . . Anchorage in space is an economico-politico form which needs to be studied in detail" (149).

mapmakers and historians: Its geography is the immense "Loneliness" Emily Dickinson renders in a poem:

> The Loneliness One dare not sound—
> And would as soon surmise
> As in its Grave go plumbing
> To ascertain the size—
>
> The Loneliness whose worst alarm
> Is lest itself should see—
> And perish from before itself
> For just a scrutiny—
>
> The Horror not to be surveyed—
> But skirted in the Dark—
> With Consciousness suspended—
> And Being under Lock—
>
> I fear me this—is Loneliness—
> The Maker of the soul
> Its Caverns and its Corridors
> Illuminate—or seal—
>
> (*Complete Poems* no. 777)

King sensed this same loneliness—which is one with desire for the wild, the atemporal experience of endless distances. His perception placed him in constant inner conflict with the institutional project in which he was participating.

The most instructive—and indeed most humorous—example of this opposition in *Mountaineering* occurs in King's portrayal of the tension between himself and the paleontologist Gabb, who accused him of daydreaming at the expense of science. "Can it be?" King asks himself, "has a student of geology so far forgotten his devotion to science? Am I really fallen to the level of a mere nature-lover?" (193). Eros, apparently, made King's fellow scientists nervous. He then proceeds to recount, tongue in cheek, his discovery of the fossil—"a plump and pampered cephalopoda (if it is a cephalopoda)"—that determined the age of the gold-bearing rocks, thus redeeming his reputation as a scientist.

Down the perspective of years I could see before me spectacled wise men of some scientific society, and one who pronounced my obituary, ending thus: "In summing up the character and labors of this fallen follower of science, let it never be forgotten that he discovered the cephalopoda"; and perhaps, I mused, they will put over me a slab of fossil rain-drops, those eternally embalmed tears of nature. (195)

If we move past the irony in this passage, we find King once again resorting to the strategic use of history. First of all, he determines that the age of the fossil is "important" because it will aid industrialists in locating sites of valuable minerals; history is being employed to actualize economic power. Secondly, King—despite his mock-heroic tone—is very much concerned with how history will treat him. In an 1877 address to his alma mater, he says, devoid of any irony: "I have hoped, too, that other graduates might feel as I have, and that year by year men might stand here, fresh from the battle-field of life, out of the very heat of the strife, to tell us of their struggles, and hang the shields they have won along the walls of this temple of science" ("Catastrophism and Evolution" 450). If King did regard his scientific life as a "battle-field," it was in all likelihood a result of the Heraclitean conflicts in his own soul: art versus science, nature versus industry, savage versus civilized, myth versus history, SPACE versus time.

These antinomies raging within may have inspired his mountain climbs in the same way that Petrarch was inspired in the fourteenth century. The Italian's description of his ascent of Mont Ventoux in 1336, one of the earliest examples in Western civilization of climbing a peak for the sheer pleasure of it, is framed in the form of a letter to his former confessor. The letter actually embodies a meditation on past and future actions, thus translating mountaineering into catharsis. Petrarch simply has something he wants to get off his chest: "Less than three years have passed since that perverse and guilty desire that totally possessed me, reigning without opposition in my heart's chambers, began to find a champion struggling against it. Between the two impulses a grueling battle has long been fought in my mind by the two men within me, and the outcome is still uncertain" (Petrarch 48). King himself was plagued by a similar opposition and might have profited from Petrarch quoting from Augustine's *Confessions*, the book he carried with him (in mind anyway) on his ascent of Mont Ventoux: "Men go to admire the high mountains and the great flood of the seas and the wide-rolling rivers and the ring of Ocean and the movements of the stars; and they abandon themselves!" (49). King, like Petrarch, feared abandoning himself to the wild.

Despite his fear, King the scientist, future director of the Fortieth Parallel Survey, voiced in his personal notebook of 1869: "The intense yearning I feel to get through my analytical study of nature and drink in the sympathetic side of myself" (King Papers, HEH D-17). He expresses a similar sentiment in the public voice of *Mountaineering*:

> I was delighted to ride thus alone, and expose myself, as one uncovers a sensitized photographic plate, to be influenced; for this is a respite from scientific work, when through months you hold yourself accountable for seeing everything, for analyzing, for instituting perpetual comparison, and as it were sharing in the administering of the physical world. No tongue can tell the relief to simply withdraw scientific observation, and let Nature impress you in the dear old way with all her mystery and glory, with those vague indescribable emotions which tremble between wonder and sympathy. (142)

King clearly needs a vacation. He is quite critical of the relentlessly analytical methodology of his fellow scientists. Perhaps, had he taken the opportunity, he would have enjoyed spending some time with John Muir in Yosemite.

King did at last make his break from the "administering of the physical world" when he tendered his surprise resignation from the U.S.G.S. directorship in 1881, but even this seemed to provide little psychological resolution for him. In 1888, he published an essay that sharply criticized the vacuously analytical pedagogy of classical education which was then the norm in American schools and universities. "No art can be taught by analysis," he asserts in "Artium Magister" (373). In directing all of his barbs at classical education, King apparently forgets or denies that he himself had criticized science in exactly the same way. The following words apply as much to the State's "managing" of nature as they do to the teaching of Latin and Greek:

Imagine a people who all the summer days, by every river bank, along the cool marge of crystal lakes, and wherever sand and sea-coves found each other, were gravely to maintain costly schools of *analytical* swimming, where instructors, year by year, went through the solemn farce of teaching the picked youth of a nation to swim on tables. The command of the academic curriculum to-day is: "plunge not in the cool flood; float not in the gay ripples of the softly-moving ebb; dive not down into the olive-dark shadows under canopy of river-loving trees; but solemnly and all together, in divisions and classes, under the eye according to the will of the pedagogues who have never been ducked, put your young stomachs on the regulation pine-table, wait for your tutor to call your name, then kick! swim! struggle! go through the prescribed motions, till the next victim is signaled. (374)

The life and work of this geologist-writer exemplify the psychological phenomenon that Paul de Man has identified as "blindness and insight"—King lashes out most insightfully at those foibles in others that he unwittingly harbors in himself. Enantiodromia once again.

## An Archaean Eros

The same enigmatic quality that pervades King's professional life courses through his romantic life as well. His loves, it would seem, were all subterranean, whether in his study of geology or in his relationship with women. One of the important conclusions King reached in his survey of the fortieth parallel was that "beneath our America lies buried another distinct continent,—an archaean America," what we might identify as a terrestrial Atlantis ("Catastrophism and Evolution" 454). Although geologists today give little credence to this particular view, we can infer from King's "archaean America" a metaphor for his own buried life; his discussion of ancient catastrophic processes becomes emblematic of the hydrology of desire: "The work of erosion which has been carried on by torrents of the Quaternary age—that is to say, within the human period—brings to light buried primeval chains far loftier than any of the present heights of the globe" (455). What torrents raged beneath the surface of Clarence King? What lofty mountains lay buried?

To say merely that King's attitude toward women was "prob-lematic" would be to gloss over statements such as the following, occurring near the conclusion of the 1888 essay, "Artium Magis-ter," which he published in the *North American Review*:

> But, consider the heroines of realistic fiction for the past thirty years; all, it is to be assumed, more or less true to the human model. Think of all the stunted and petty women and their incredible meanness; of the primeval, monkey-scale of their average intelligence; remember how few wholesome, sweet, strong women are found in that army of distorted, displeased creatures who march between the covers of Eng-lish fiction, laden down as they go with all the tragi-comic foibles flesh is heir to, and all the conceivable deviations from noble and normal womanhood; and then reflect how French realism has flung woman naked in the ditch and left her there scorned of men, and grinning in cynical and shameless levity over her own dishonor. Or, to come nearer home, recall the pretty, brightish, smug little people who are made with inimitable skill to illustrate the sawdust stuffing of middle-class democratic society. (383)

His apparent misogyny is inseparable from the criticism he is level-ing at his culture, and his disdain stems from an acute disappoint-ment in failing to find a woman who corresponded with the image, however unrealistic, that he harbored of the "ideal" woman.

King, it would seem, was responding to his own idealization, which bears comparison to what Barbara Welter describes as the "cult of true womanhood":

> The nineteenth-century American man was a busy builder of bridges and railroads, at work long hours in a materialistic society. The reli-gious values of his forebears were neglected in practice if not in in-tent, and he occasionally felt some guilt that he had turned this new land, this temple of the chosen people, into one vast countinghouse. But he could salve his conscience by reflecting that he had left be-hind a hostage, not only to fortune, but to all the values which he held so dear and treated so lightly. Woman, in the cult of True Wom-anhood presented by the women's magazines, gift annuals and reli-gious literature of the nineteenth century, was the hostage in the home. In a society where values changed frequently, where fortunes rose and fell with frightening rapidity, where social and economic mobility provided instability as well as hope, one thing at least re-

mained the same—a true woman was a true woman, wherever she was found. (Welter 40)

King found his "true woman" outside the bounds of contemporary Euro-American culture, a woman who was in fact "superior" to the male. King reaches far back into history, indeed into myth itself, to find a woman in Western culture who meets his expectations:

> Out of it all is there one figure for weary eyes to linger upon: one type of large and satisfying womanhood; natural in the rare and ravishing charm of a perfect body; sweet with the endowment of a warm, quick, sympathetic temperament; sound and bright in intellect; pure and spiritual, with a soul in whose pellucid depths fixed stars of the moral heaven reflect themselves, undimmed by mists of earth, untrembling from the jar of modern conflict? Is there any more womanhood in them all, English, French, and American put together and fused into one, than can be learned in a single hour before that Greek Venus in the Louvre, who is only perfect goddess because she is perfect woman? Is there not in this one ideal, with her rich femininity, her Doric strength, the calm warmth of her countenance, the supple pose of her vital body, and that irradiating aura of love which enfolds her with its mysterious veil, more of human nature than one can patch together out of all the thousands of photographic portraits of actual, but distorted and incomplete character, that crowd modern fiction? ("Artium Magister" 383)

Henry Adams noted that "in his instincts I think he regarded the male as a sort of defence thrown off by the female, much like a shell of a crab, endowed with no original energy of his own; but it was not the modern woman that interested him; it was the archaic female, with instincts and without intellect. At best King had but a poor opinion of intellect, chiefly because he found it so defective an instrument, but he admitted that it was all the male had to live upon; while the female was rich in the inheritance of every animated energy back to the polyps and the crystals" (Hague 172). When we recognize that King was committed to an essentialist view of the female that consigns her to a position that is "close to nature," that he in all likelihood suffered from what Jungian psychologists would call an "anima complex," the course of his erotic life seems less enigmatic and more inevitable.

At age twenty-six, King became engaged to a Miss Dean, a schoolteacher whom he always referred to as "Deany," but the engagement was inexplicably broken off the following year. A story survives that the woman simply did not get along with King's mother, Mrs. Howland, but in the context of the above remarks it is more likely that even at this relatively young age his contorted views of white American women—combined with the fact that they were in his mind inextricably linked with "vulgar, but remarkably active civilization . . . and the struggle for material good" ("Artium Magister" 383)—made him reluctant to sanction this relationship in the eyes of institutional authority. James D. Hague reports that King "held a somewhat unusual view concerning one's obligation to perform certain promises, especially marriage engagements, of which, in a somewhat earnest discussion of the matter, he once said, 'I would never marry a woman anyhow, *just because I said I would.* That is the poorest possible reason men or women can ever have for marrying each other. People who marry without any better reason than that must surely come to grief'" (Hague 383). For King, it was the same old ambivalence, the one that informed all his other relationships, whether with humans or with nature.

In counterpoint stands his relationship with an Indian woman named Luciana ("as near as Eve as can be") whom he met at Rancho Camulos, California, in 1887. King was strongly attracted to her, as he confessed to his friend John Hay in a letter rich in romantic imagery: "I escaped from her by a miracle of self-control. I rode with [her] alone in the mountains among the straying cattle. The world was all flowers, and Luciana's face was the most tender and grave image of Indian womanhood within human conception." Then, as Thurman Wilkins tells the story, "The two reined in their horses at a mountain spring, among live oaks dewy with fog from the nearby Pacific, while orange poppies blazed in the grass. They dismounted, and gazed out over the gray ocean; 'and then,' King wrote, 'I came as near it as I ever shall'" (Wilkins 354).[10] King, perhaps as a result of his essentialist beliefs about women, was capable of loving only when there was a convergence

---

10. Wilkins further reports: "Luciana would haunt King's thoughts for a long time thereafter and her name would crop up in more than one subsequent letter."

between the beloved and nature itself, in this case between the Indian woman and the ocean.

Yet King was not without his ambivalence even toward Indian women. In *Mountaineering*, he writes, perhaps pandering to the expectations of his East Coast audience:

> These Indian faces are fairly good-natured, especially when young. I visited one camp, upon the left river bank, finding Madam at home seated by her fireside engaged in maternal duties. I am almost afraid to describe the squalor and grotesque hideousness of her person. She was emaciated and scantily clad in a sort of short petticoat, shaggy, unkempt hair overhanging a pair of wild wolf's eyes. The ribs and collar-bone stood out as upon an anatomical specimen; hard black flesh clinging in formless masses upon her body and arms. Altogether she had the appearance of an unimated mummy. Her child, a mere amorphous roll, clung to her, and emphasized, with cubbish fatness, the wan, shrunken form of its mother, looking like some ravenous leech which was draining the woman's very blood. Shuddering, I hurried away to observe the husband. (238)

The aversion King expresses in this passage echoes what he felt toward the male Indian at the foot of Whitney, but the harshness of his tone in regard to the female is curious, given his predilection for the "archaic woman," and it is particularly curious when we consider the disdain he harbored for the educated white women in his audience. As Henry Adams reports in his *Education*, "King had no faith in the American woman; he loved types more robust" (313). In a letter to Adams, King admits he actually found white women physically repulsive: "To kiss a woman and feel teeth through her thin lips paralyzes me for a week." That he is specifically referring to Caucasian women becomes apparent as he continues: "This snarl is because I am just in from passing Sunday at Tuxedo [New York], and my grievance is that I didn't want to kiss the beings there. Their little minds squirm and contract under the [stimulus] of light and conversation, as a dead frog curls up his wiry toes at the galvanic touch, but I am not deceived by their involuntary simulation of life: I know they are dead" (qtd. in Wilkins 359). Whatever the source of his ambivalence toward women, it is in keeping with his one consistency: inconsistency. This is the same Clarence King who reminds himself to show all the respect he can muster for nature, while at the same time cleaning his gun for the "sport" of killing a grizzly.

A year after his encounter with Luciana he would secretly marry an African-American woman named Ada. "He revealed neither his true name nor his occupation to [her], but borrowed the given name of his father and called himself James Todd in her presence, and she would not learn for many years that his rightful name was Clarence King" (363). He kept his wife and the five children they eventually had together sequestered in an apartment in Brooklyn, far from the circles of high society he frequented in Manhattan. "For the sake of your darling babies we must keep this secret of our love and our lives from the world," he wrote to her in a letter (Wilkins 385). (Ironically, this letter and many others would be published in newspapers for all the world to see in the 1930s, when Ada pressed a lawsuit to collect what she imagined was a trust fund King had set up for her; sadly, no such fund existed.) Wilkins speculates that King maintained such secrecy in order to avoid a "scandal that would be a grievous embarrassment to his friends and family" (362). Whatever the reason, King was forced to live his most intimate human relationship in the same way he lived his relationship to nature: underground.

### The Catastrophic Imagination

When he was a young man, King is reported to have said to Mrs. Howland: "Mother, I *must* write a novel." When she expressed doubt that his experience as a geologist was the proper background for a novelist, he countered with the claim that geology had been the "best training conceivable in constructive imagination." Even better grist for the novelist's mill would have been tremendous ambivalences of his emotional life and the keen sense of paradox he developed as a result. King never got around to completing any novel, but he did frame a theory of the imagination that seems a fitting product of his wild, embattled psyche.

On September 20, 1863, somewhere in the vicinity of Downieville, California, he wrote in his personal notebook:

> I have read in Revelations of the passing away of the earth and all the beauty and grandeur of it. I read too of a new heaven and a new earth, beautiful in type. Well then, if this is transitory, why study so hard into all the intricate mazes of fact, which will be swept away and known no more? I look for lessons. . . . [God] scented all things with design . . . lessons were taught in nature which were not elsewhere, not as important as the "law," but still vital. (King Papers, HEH D-23)

This is the twenty-one-year-old Clarence King, still very much under the influence of his Christian upbringing, but already his interest in things eschatological has blossomed. As he matured, he would transfer an important quota of imaginative energy from the doctrines of Christianity to those of geology, but the tenor of his interest would remain in the doomsday mode.

In an important essay engaging the geological debate of Uniformitarianism versus Catastrophism, King came down solidly in the camp of the latter. Uniformitarianism, sometimes referred to as Lyell's Hypothesis, can be defined as that school of geology that believes "the present is the key to the past." This school "postulates that the laws of nature that now prevail have always prevailed and that, accordingly, the results of processes now active resemble like processes of the past." Catastrophism, on the other hand, is a "hypothesis that proffers recurrent, violent, worldwide events as the reason for sudden disappearance of some species and the abrupt rise of new ones."[11] King is best described as a modified catastrophist, a precursor to current scientific theorists who characterize evolutionary change in terms of "punctuated equilibrium," as opposed to some form of gradualism.[12] "The earliest geological induction of primeval man," he writes, "is the doctrine of terrestrial catastrophe. This ancient belief has its roots in the actual experience of man, who himself has been witness of certain terrible and destructive exhibitions of sudden, unusual telluric energy" ("Catastrophism and Evolution" 450).

King's theory is actually Heraclitean ("War engenders all") in

---

11. See Lapidus, *Dictionary of Geology and Geophysics.*
12. See Stephen J. Gould, "Darwinism and the Expansion of Evolutionary Theory."

the violence it suggests swirls in the depths of the human psyche. "Catastrophism is therefore the survival of a terrible impression burned in upon the very substance of human memory" ("Catastrophism and Evolution" 450). Moreover, "[w]hen complete evidence of the antiquity of man in California and the catastrophes he has survived come to be generally understood, there will cease to be any wonder that a theory of the destructive in nature is an early, deeply rooted archaic belief, most powerful in its effect on the imagination." King goes so far as to link catastrophe with "the very mechanism of imagination," accusing those who subscribe to more uniformitarian views (mostly British scientists, but also John Muir) as lacking in imagination. "They suffer from a species of intellectual near-sightedness too lamentably common among all grades and professions of men. They are bounded—I might almost say imprisoned—by the evident facts and ideas of their own to-day and their own environment." In summary, King tells us that "[m]en are born either catastrophists or uniformitarians. You may divide the race into imaginative people who believe in all sorts of impending crises,—physical, social, political,—and others who anchor their very souls *in statu quo*" (451). King should have appended psychological crises to his list.

Regardless of the contemporary scientific assessment of the "accuracy" of King's science, his formulation of the catastrophic imagination is personally revealing. Fifteen years later, he would employ in another essay the same catastrophic perspective:

> The human organism has rarely been subjected to a severer test than the study of scientific problems, nor is there a truer hero than an investigator who never loses heart in a life-long grapple with the powers of the universe. It requires courage of the highest order to stand for years face to face with one of the enigmas of nature; to interrogate patiently, and hear no answers, to try all known methods and weapons of attack, and yet see the lips of the sphinx compressed in stony immobility; to invoke the uttermost powers of imagination; to fuse the very soul in the fire of effort, and still press the listening ear against the wall of silence. It is easier to die in the breach. ("Education of the Future" 26)

This passage can barely contain itself, jostling with its violent cavalcade of military and sexual imagery, all sublimated into the pursuit of science. (It is interesting to note that the greatest source of anxiety here is "silence"—as if anything could be endured save that.) With his chronic ambivalence, King located creativity's origins in upheaval. "Catastrophism and Evolution" can be read as a geological origins-myth:

> The pre-human history of the planet has been variously estimated in time, from two days—the period assigned by the Koran—to an indefinite extension of ages. The globe, having cooled from a condition of igneous fluidity received upon its surface of congealed primitive rock the condensed aerial waters, which formed at first a general oceanic envelope, swathing the whole earth. Out of this universal sea emerged continents; and as soon as the temperature and atmospheric conditions were suitable, low organisms, both of the vegetable and animal kingdoms, were created, and the complex machinery of life set in successful motion. (452)

Nevertheless, there is nothing particularly radical in this myth, a mere graft of geology upon Genesis—as suggested in King's use of the passive voice ("were created") to mark the place wherein the Judeo-Christian God could still work his magic *ex nihilo*. So much for catastrophe.

Toward the end of the essay, King writes his own version of Revelation, this time bringing to bear a progressivist version of evolution, explaining that the "He"

> who brought to bear that mysterious energy we call life upon primeval matter bestowed at the same time a power of development by change, arranging that the interaction of energy and matter which make up environment should, from time to time, burst in upon the current of life and sweep it onward and upward to ever higher and better manifestations. Moments of great catastrophe, thus translated in the language of life, become moments of creation, when out of plastic organisms something newer and nobler is called into being. (470)

For King, this is his recurrent problem of blindness and insight. After opening his essay by condemning those uniformitarians who "lack the very mechanism of imagination," reproaching them for timidity in the face of revolution, he concludes as do so many versions of evolutionism—by proffering a warmed-over version of traditional Christian eschatology. Thus, King backs away from the threshold of potentially wild insight. In the end he was an extremist, not a revolutionary; he never undergoes a "conversion" that would translate into a meaningful unselfing of the self. Instead, he suffers a nervous breakdown and winds up in an asylum.

King's catastrophic imagination is the nineteenth-century extension of what Sacvan Bercovitch has identified as the American Puritan imagination. King, like the early American Puritans, was an interpreter of a landscape imbued with divinity. Bercovitch submits that "the interpretation of the actual-yet-spiritual wilderness leads out to what might be called the genre of American natural theology—the concern with the New World landscape as a source of higher laws, a key to the golden future, and a proof-by-association of the interpreter's spiritual regeneration" (*American Puritan Imagination* 36). To a certain extent, all texts that take the wild as their subject matter are conversion narratives, deeply engrossed in spiritual regeneration. However, unlike the Puritan writers who try to represent a spiritual event that manifests itself in the material world, writers of the wild tend to blur and often erase altogether the boundary between spiritual and material—the worlds are one in the same. This, it would seem, is the lesson of liminality, a lesson that proved too elusive for Clarence King.

King, like the Puritans themselves, was never able to reconcile the interior of his own mind, his catastrophic imagination, with the exterior of the American land. In this sense, we could say there is a touch of the schizophrenic about him, literally a (*schiz-*) "broken" + (*phrenos-*) literally "diaphragm," where the ancients believed the soul to reside, thus "heart, soul, or mind." In the same year that the second edition of *Mountaineering* made its appearance (1874), Friedrich Nietzsche, the nineteenth century's great malcontent, was writing in Germany: "In the end, modern man drags around with him a huge quantity of indigestible stones of knowledge, which then, as in the fairy tale, can sometimes be heard rumbling about inside him. And in this rumbling there is betrayed the most characteristic quality of modern man: the remarkable antithesis between an interior which fails to correspond to any exterior and an exterior which fails to correspond to any interior—an antithesis unknown to peoples of earlier times" (*Untimely Meditations* 78). Thus, it is difficult to agree with Stegner's assessment that King failed for want of character—rather, we must say he died of a broken heart (*schiz-* / *phrenos*).

### The Elusive Mount Whitney

D. H. Lawrence once wrote that "the nearer a conception comes towards finality, the nearer does the dynamic relation, out of which this concept has arisen, draw to a close. To know is to lose" (*Psychoanalysis* 108). *To know is to lose* would have made a fitting epitaph for Clarence King. In exploring and naming the Sierra Nevada through the vehicle of nineteenth-century science, he lost it. But then again, it was always just escaping him—as his experience with the range's highest peak was to prove.

From the top of Mount Bullion in the vicinity of Mariposa during the winter of 1863–64, King first espied the group of mountains he suspected contained the "highest land." "For a couple of months," he tells us in *Mountaineering*, "my friends had made me the target of plenty of pleasant banter about my 'highest land,' which they lost faith in as we climbed from Thomas's Mill." Then, at the beginning of July 1864, from the summit of the peak they called Mount Brewer, King's companions identified toward the southeast the same high group of mountains that King had seen earlier from the foothills. "They had spent hours upon the summit scanning the eastern horizon, and ranging downward into the labyrinth of gulfs below, and had come at last with reluctance to the belief that to cross this gorge and ascend the eastern wall of peaks was utterly impossible" (70). This, of course, was all the incentive King needed to request permission to make an attempt to cross this difficult terrain; he and his companion, Dick Cotter, started out on their trek the next day. King, on the shoulder of Mount Brewer, describes the journey that lay before them:

> Rising on the other side, cliff above cliff, precipice piled upon precipice, rock over rock, up against sky, towered the most gigantic mountain-wall in America, culminating in a noble pile of Gothic-finished granite and enamel-like snow. How grand and inviting looked its white form, its untrodden, unknown crest, so high and pure in the

clear strong blue! I looked at it as one contemplating the purpose of his life; and for just one moment I would have rather liked to dodge that purpose, or to have waited, or have found some excellent reason why I might not go; but all this quickly vanished, leaving a cheerful resolve to go ahead. (74)

The purpose of King's life, at least at this point, was "to reach the highest peak in the range," his personal equivalent of the Delectable Mountains that drew Bunyan's Christian on his pilgrimage. King and Cotter promptly headed off in the appropriate direction. Two days and a hair-raising climb over the Great Western Divide later, the two men stood on the summit of what they believed to be the highest mountain in the land.

If we are to believe King's account in *Mountaineering* (and there are good reasons to suspect his ingenuousness), the essay's concluding sentence is the climax: "I rang my hammer upon the topmost rock; we grasped hands, and I reverently named the grand peak MOUNT TYNDALL" (94). The following chapter (actually a sequel) picks up where the previous one left off, immediately providing a twist to the tale:

> To our surprise, upon sweeping the horizon with my level, there appeared two peaks equal in height with us, and two rising even higher. That which looked highest of all was a cleanly cut helmet of granite upon the same ridge with Mount Tyndall, lying about six miles south, and fronting the desert with a bold square bluff which rises to the crest of the peak, where a white fold of snow trims it gracefully.
>
> Mount Whitney, as we afterwards called it in honor of our chief, is probably the highest land within the United States. Its summit looked glorious, but inaccessible. (95)

This account, peculiarly enough, does not correspond to King's own field notes. In a brown-leather field book labeled "California Geological Survey, 1864," in the Huntington Library's Clarence King Collection, the following survey data are recorded near the back of the book:

bearings from Mt Whitney

| | |
|---|---|
| Mt. Brewer | N 84.5 W |
| N. end of Table | N 77 W |

| Mt. Grant | S 42 E |
| Milestone | S 65 W |
| Hoffman's | [blank] |
| Goddard | N 51.5 W |
| Pallesads [*sic*] | N 30 W |
| high peak in desert | N 11.5 W |
| upper end of Owens Lake | S 87 1/4 E distant about 20 miles |

S 20 W runs the branch S of Mt Whitney
High group extends about 20 miles S of here
An immense valley is formed by the Kern
Mt E of Mt Whitney 100 ft. higher
    Mt. Tyndall
Mt. Grant 300 ft. higher

                      (Clarence King Papers, HEH D-4)

These bearings indicate that King, at least when he was recording them, had named the peak on which he was standing "Mount Whitney." The peak directly to the east—the one known today as Mount Williamson—actually was the one he called Tyndall. And the highest peak in the Sierra Nevada, the highest peak in the lower forty-eight states, what we today call Mount Whitney, *he named Mount Grant.* Sometime between when King named and recorded the various peaks in his field notebook and when he conveyed this information to his boss, Josiah Whitney, a migration of mountain names had occurred—Mount Whitney became Mount Tyndall; Mount Tyndall became Mount Williamson; and Mount Grant became Mount Whitney. The name "Grant" disappears from Sierran orography; though for a short and patriotic spell, the Union Army's most famous general had his cognomen attached to the highest peak in the land. My guess is that when King and Cotter returned to the survey camp, their boss—William Brewer—felt it would be more expedient to name the peak after his own boss. Given the shaky status of the survey's funding, it was best not to risk offending any secessionist sympathizers within the California legislature; thus, the names were shuffled. This suppressed metastasis of mountain names is emblematic of Clarence King's pursuit of his "highest land"—it proved so slippery that even the names he bestowed would not stick.

Following the ascent of Mount Tyndall, King accompanied Brewer, who was suffering from a toothache, back to Visalia, and from here he set out on a two-week trip to attempt a climb of the "new" Mount Whitney—by approaching it from the west along the Kern River. He records only briefly, in *Mountaineering*, that he tried "hard to climb Mount Whitney without success" (129), but his field notes give a more detailed albeit uninteresting account of his passage west across the southern Sierra toward the peak. Of his actual climb, no precise details survive, although we know he crossed the main crest of the Sierra and attempted the peak from the difficult eastern side. Whitney himself reports: "The highest point reached by King was between 300 and 400 feet lower than the culminating point of the mountain" (qtd. in Farquhar 148). The mountaineer–historian Francis Farquhar concludes his account of King's expedition on a note that is more remarkable for its *Schadenfreude* than for its content: "It is fruitless to speculate upon the exact spot King turned back. Had he not been so obsessed with the notion of inaccessibility he might then and there have made the first ascent of Mount Whitney. But he seems to have had a genius for finding the wrong routes" (148). Thus, within the course of three weeks in 1864, King was eluded twice by his "highest land."

Seven years later it would happen again. By 1871 the peak had remained—as far as anybody knew—unclimbed by Euro-Americans, so King pitched yet another attempt, this time with apparent success. As he stands on the cloud-shrouded summit of what he believes to be Mount Whitney, King delivers a nostalgic summary of landscape and years:

> There they rose as of old, firm and solid; even the great snow-fields, though somewhat shrunken, lay as they had seven years before. I saw the peaks and passes and amphitheatres, dear old Cotter and I had climbed: even that Mount Brewer pass where we looked back over the pathway of our dangers, and up with regretful hearts to the very rock on which I sat.
>
> Deep below flowed the Kern, its hundred snow-fed branches gleaming out amid rock and ice, or traced far away in the great glacier trough by dark lines of pine. There, only twelve miles northwest, stretched that ragged divide where Cotter and I came down the

precipice with our rope. Beyond, into the vague blue of King's Cañon, sloped the ice and rock of Mount Brewer wall.

Sombre storm-clouds and their even gloomier shadows darkened the northern sea of peaks. Only a few slant bars of sudden light flashed in upon purple granite and fields of ice. The rocky tower of Mount Tyndall, thrust up through rolling billows, caught for a moment the full light, and then sank into darkness and mist. (*Mountaineering* 288)

The range remains "firm and solid," unlike King's body which was already softening with middle age.

Unfortunately—but oh so typically for Clarence King—the "rocky tower" he saw "thrust up through rolling billows" was not Mount Tyndall but the *actual* highest mountain in the range, a fact that King himself did not realize until the summer of 1873, when the geologist W. A. Goodyear, an acquaintance of King, delivered a paper entitled "On the Situation and Altitude of Mount Whitney" to the California Academy of Sciences, in a session chaired by Josiah Whitney himself. Goodyear had retraced King's route (by horse no less) up the mountain he identified in the "Mount Whitney" chapter of *Mountaineering*, only to discover: "*This peak is not Mount Whitney*" (qtd. in Farquhar 173). A peak six miles to the north—likely the one King mistook in 1871 for Mount Tyndall—loomed five hundred feet higher. "Certain it is," Goodyear writes, "that the peak which for over three years has borne the name of Whitney, has done so only by mistake, and that a new name must be found for it; while the name of Whitney must now go back to the peak to which it was originally given in 1864, and which is, in reality, the highest and grandest of this culminating cluster of the Sierra Nevada." Then, in a gleeful jibe at King's expense: "It is safe to say that no man will ever ride a horse or mule to the summit of *that* peak, unless it be by a costly as well as dangerous trail." Clarence King, once again, had climbed the wrong mountain. The peak he climbed in 1871 today bears the name of Mount Langley, and to give King full credit, had the clouds not obscured his view he would have readily seen that the "real" Mount Whitney lay to the north.

Given the elusiveness of Mount Whitney, how might this be emblematic of King's entire experience with the wild? Keep in mind how King began his first attempt at this highest land, look-ing "at it as one contemplating the purpose of his life." That pur-pose constantly eluded him—namely, to somehow *know* the wild, to name it, to contain it, and indeed perhaps even to be loved by it. His is the story of frustrated desire. Emily Dickinson, in one of her many poems that evoke the landscape of desire, concludes:

> But nature is a stranger yet;
> The ones that cite her most
> Have never passed her haunted house,
> Nor simplified her ghost.
>
> To pity those that know her not
> Is helped by the regret
> That those who know her, know her less
> The nearer her they get.
>
> (*Complete Poems* no. 1400)

*Mountaineering* is King's attempt to reactivate a symbolic value—of desire—in scientific discourse. That he was not fully committed to this project or was simply not entirely prepared for it must remain moot, but as one branch of postmodern psychology renders it: "The scientist as such has no revolutionary potential; he is the first integrated agent of integration, a refuge for bad con-science, and the *forced* destroyer of his own creativity" (Deleuze and Guattari 236). If King was the forced destroyer of his own cre-ativity, Mount Whitney—thereby the wild—simply becomes an-other one of the unconscious elements conspiring against him. On one level, the "highest land" becomes representative of an inflated ego, King's, but on another level it becomes a symbol for the fully actualized self predicated upon a dissolution of the ego. That King did not become the first Euro-American to ascend the "real" Mount Whitney proved to be a personal humiliation; in a more tragic sense, it signifies his failure to achieve self-actualization.

Shortly after reading Goodyear's article, King made a special trip to the southern Sierra and climbed the peak that we today call Mount Whitney:

> This is the true Mount Whitney, the one we named in 1864, and upon which the name of our chief is forever to rest. It stands, not like white Shasta, in a grandeur of solitude, but about it gather companies

of crag and spire, piercing the blue or wrapped in monkish raiment of snow-storm and mist. Far below, laid out in ashen death, slumbers the desert. (*Mountaineering* 304)

King's description haunts its reader with melancholy, especially when we consider that this was in all likelihood the last climb he ever made in the Sierra. Placed near the end of the fourth edition of *Mountaineering*, it subsumes the volume in a sad atmosphere of anticlimax:

> The day was cloudless and the sky, milder than is common over these extreme heights, warmed to a mellow glow and rested in softening beauty over minaret and dome. Air and light seemed melted together; even the wild rocks springing up all about us wore an aspect of aerial delicacy. Round the wide panorama, half low desert, half rugged granite mountains, each detail was observable, but a uniform luminous medium toned, without obscuring, the field of vision. That fearful sense of wreck and desolation, of a world crushed into fragments, of the ice chisel which, unseen, has wrought this strange mountain sculpture, all the sensations of power and tragedy I had invariably felt before on high peaks, were totally forgotten. It was the absolute reverse of the effect on Mount Tyndall, where an unrelenting clearness discovered every object in all its power and reality. Then we saw only unburied wreck of geologic struggles, black with sudden shadow or white under searching focus, as if the sun were a great burning-glass, gathering light from all space, and hurling its fierce shafts upon spire and wall. (303)

Just behind the aestheticism of this passage lay suggestions of what might be described as—if not enlightenment—a coming to terms with a side of himself that he had previously projected out upon the Sierra mountainscape: that impetuous, egoistic side of his youth. By now, in September 1873, he had not only belatedly succeeded in attaining the highest land, but his fieldwork for the Survey of the Fortieth Parallel was coming to a close—and with it his "outdoor life." This passage, perhaps more than any other one, glosses the epigraph King chose for the book: *Altiora petimus*—"We strive for higher things." For the remainder of his years, his strivings, his desire, would be directed not toward the wild but toward the dollar bill—he would become a cattle baron, a government bureaucrat, an investor in mines that never paid out.

King often remarked that his time spent with the California survey was the happiest of his life, a sentiment that tempers the 1874 preface he composed in New York City for the fourth edition of *Mountaineering.* "There are turning-points in all men's lives which must give them both pause and retrospect," he tells his readers, then goes on to transform mountaineering into a metaphor for life:

> With a lingering look [the mountaineer] starts forward, and the closing pass-gate with its granite walls shuts away the retrospect, yet the delightful picture forever after hangs on the gallery wall of memory. It is thus with me about mountaineering; the pass which divides youth from manhood is traversed, and the serious service of science must hereafter claim me. But as the cherished memories of Sierra climbs go ever with me, I may not lack the inspiring presence of sunlit snow nor the calming influence of those broad noble views. It is the mountaineer's privilege to carry through life his wealth of unfading treasure. At his summons the white peaks loom above him as of old; the camp-fire burns once more for him, his study walls recede in twilight revery, and around him are gathered again stately columns of pine. (*Mountaineering,* 4th ed., p. x)

It is a high price this pilgrim pays for his progress.

And so we leave Clarence King where we found him, on the floor of the Owens Valley, gazing at his highest, most delectable land, forevermore trembling on the edge of mythmaking.

FIVE

# Mary Austin's Gleanings of the Wild

> *"If the way I have shown to lead to these things now seems*
> *very hard, still, it can be found. And of course, what is found*
> *so rarely must be hard. For if salvation were at hand, and*
> *could be found without great effort, how could nearly everyone*
> *neglect it? But all things excellent are as difficult as they are*
> *rare."*
>
> —Spinoza, *Ethics*

### The Reluctant Pilgrim 1888–1905

Mary Hunter Austin was not a pilgrim to the wild by choice.
When her widowed mother, Susanna Savilla Graham Hunter, de-
cided in 1888 to move the family from Illinois to the desert lands
of southern California, twenty-year-old Mary was not consulted.
"Not that she greatly cared; she did not see how being in one State
or another would affect her own plan to earn a living teaching
until such a time as her writing would support her" (EH 177). She
never suffered the sort of wanderlust that characterized the lives of
men such as John Muir and Clarence King, or the lives of the tens
of thousands who came seeking their gold and silver fortunes in
the arid ranges of the American West, the sort of men who (to
paraphrase Seneca) travel widely to different sorts of places in
search of different distractions because they are fickle, tired of soft
living, and always seeking after something that eludes them. Mary
Hunter Austin, more like Thoreau in this regard, wanted merely
"to write books you could walk around in" (73). Unlike Thoreau,
however, and unlike all the writers I have been considering until
now, Mary Austin was a woman. This makes all the difference.

Austin tells us in her autobiography that the reason her mother,
comparatively late in life, uprooted her family from its comfortable
surroundings in a midwestern college town was that she "had always wanted another sort of life for herself." Indeed, Austin writes,
"[i]t was what most women wanted; time and adventure of their

123

own" (177). This was an ornery notion for an American woman in
the nineteenth century, an age dominated, according to one historian, by "the cult of true womanhood" and the strict standards "by
which a woman judged herself and was judged by her husband, her
neighbors and society." The four cardinal virtues of true womanhood were piety, purity, submissiveness, and domesticity. "Put
them all together and they spelled mother, daughter, sister, wife—
woman. Without them, no matter whether there was fame,
achievement or wealth, all was ashes" (Welter 21). The nineteenth-century American female was born into sequestration,
closed off entirely from what Carolyn Heilbrun describes as "the
freedom of male experience and possibility" (Heilbrun 97). Heilbrun reminds us: "Safety and closure, which have always been held
out to women as the ideals of feminine destiny, are not places of
adventure, or experience, or life" (20). Austin's mother made her
remarkable break "[a]gainst all advice." Her response to critics: "I
served my time at staying at home when my children were little.
Now I mean to enjoy myself" (EH 177) Mother was setting an example for daughter; however, the two never got along—they probably had too much in common.[1]

Mary Austin, like her mother, wanted "adventures" of her own
design. Unfortunately for her, such longings were in direct opposition to the social institutions and norms that thwarted desire in
the female. "It doesn't seem fair," Austin said through a fictional
voice in 1912. "Nobody told me about it when I was a girl; I think
nobody tells girls. They just have to sort of find it out; and if they
don't, nobody cares. All they told me was about being good, and
you will be happy; but it isn't so. There is a great deal more to it
than that, and it seems as if people ought to know. . . . I have wild
thoughts sometimes,—such as men have when they go out and

---

1. Austin's most recent biographer has written: "Perhaps the biggest lack in
Austin's life was a rich and meaningful connection with her mother. Her account
of this crucial relationship in *Earth Horizon* gives resonance to Adrienne Rich's
contemporary analysis of the mother-daughter relationship fraught with possibilities 'for the deepest mutuality and the most painful estrangement.' Austin repeat-
edly turns to her mother only to find the relationship empty of understanding; at
every significant crisis when she seeks tenderness or advice, she meets criticism or
rebuff." Stineman, *Mary Austin* (211).

snatch things,—but it wouldn't do me any good" (qtd. in Graulich 235). When Thoreau, Muir, or King had their wild thoughts or dreamed their wild dreams they were able to go out and "snatch" them—walk away, wander west, and track their bliss. They lived what some might refer to as counter-cultural lives. Nineteenth-century American society could accommodate such idiosyncratic lifestyles—in men. It was men—not women—Wallace Stegner had in mind when he wrote: "It should not be denied . . . that being footloose has always exhilarated us. It is associated in our minds with escape from history and oppression and law and irksome obligations, with absolute freedom, and the road has always led west. Our folk heroes and our archetypal literary figures accurately reflect that side of us" (Stegner, *American West* 22). But does such a generalization accurately reflect the experience of women? It certainly doesn't reflect the experience of Mary Austin.

Austin's life and work are notably different from the other nineteenth-century writers of the wild we have been considering. She was a woman who was, at least to some degree, brought to the wild against her will. The wilderness in which she found herself isolated was nothing like the forested, well-watered landscapes of New England or the western slope of the Sierra Nevada, but a desolate and inhospitable expanse of desert, punctuated by sordid little mining towns. By comparison, Thoreau's "excursions" were recreational; John Muir's meanderings were those of a privileged vagabond; and Clarence King's geological aestheticism was dilettantish. In their writings, these men usually confine themselves to what sarcastically might be called the holiday side of the wild. Mary Austin, on the other hand, is most profoundly aware of the "shadow side" of the wild—its dark, brooding, and, indeed, threatening aspects, those that undermine the foundations of society and even the integrity of the individual self. Although Austin does perceive the "beauty" in the wild, she never denies its polarity. Opposition is true friendship—and true community. This is the great lesson Austin learned in the desert wild. Readers agree that her most engaging books are those about the land—specifically, *The Land of Little Rain* (1903) and *Lost Borders* (1909)—but a close look at these works reveals their subject is actually the land's effect upon the human individual and community. In this sense, Mary

Austin is the most sociologically insightful of all the nineteenth-century writers of the wild.

Austin was a born writer and chose writing as her career, despite all the obstacles, which were many. Among the elements conspiring against her were these: she was a woman in the nineteenth century; she was aggressively discouraged by her mother; she suffered the indifference of her husband; she was overwhelmed with the responsibility of caring for a handicapped child; and she was living in the artistically stultifying environment of remote desert mining towns. Years later, in describing the composition of *The Land of Little Rain*, she wrote: "To understand what the writing of this, my maiden book, meant to me, you must realize that up to that time, and for many years afterwards, I was living in a California town of about three hundred inhabitants, and, with the exception of the middle Western college town of about six thousand, it was the only kind of town I had ever known. . . . Happily, I did not know enough to know that this was not the atmosphere out of which books were supposed to be written. I confidently expected to produce books. For twelve years I had lived deeply and absorbedly in the life of the desert" (Hart 63). In her lifetime, she published over thirty books, contributed more than two hundred essays to magazines and journals, wrote and directed several plays, and, as her health permitted, maintained a busy lecture schedule. Hers, more than Muir, King, and even Thoreau, was a life devoted entirely to letters.

Austin lived in the California deserts from 1888 to 1905, and although these were rich years in the development of her creativity they were intensely unhappy for her. She published *The Land of Little Rain* in 1903, and then in 1905 she relocated, free of her family responsibilities at last, to Carmel. She wrote her way out of the wilderness. For the remainder of her life she would migrate about literary and cultural centers—Carmel, New York, London, Rome, Santa Fe—but never again would she live under the conditions she knew in the south San Joaquin and Owens valleys of California, conditions—troubling as they were—that nurtured her creativity. Nevertheless, it was during these years of reluctant pilgrimage that she learned to express the power of desolate places.

## The Power of Desolate Places

The experiential quality of the wild is presence.[2] It is an experience that is rare enough in urban culture, and little valued, but there have always been those who seek it. Thoreau, King, Muir, and Ruess all sought it in their long journeys. Mary Austin, at least in her younger years, did not have to seek the presence—it came to her. She was naturally adept at the practice of the wild.

In her autobiography, *Earth Horizon* (1932), she recounts how she became "happily absorbed" with the Great American Desert as it rolled past the train windows during her family's journey from Illinois to California in 1888. "All that long stretch between Salt Lake and Sacramento Pass, the realization of presence which the desert was ever after to have for her, grew upon her mind; not the warm tingling presence of wooded hills and winding creeks, but something brooding and aloof, charged with a dire indifference, of which she was never for an instant afraid" (182). Of course, this is the sixty-four-year-old Austin looking back on herself at the age of twenty, so the account, as we shall see, is not entirely frank—especially in her claim to have been free from fear—but what does emerge here, a consistent theme throughout her lifework, is her insistence on the *experiential quality* of the wild. Although she knew that words were not up to the task of conveying such experience, she nevertheless continued to attempt its articulation.

A few pages later in *Earth Horizon*, we find this account of her journey north by wagon from Los Angeles to Tejon through San Fracisquito Canyon:

> There was something else there besides what you find in the books; a lurking, evasive Something, wistful, cruel, ardent; something that rustled and ran, that hung half-remotely, insistent on being noticed, fled from pursuit, and when you turned from it, leaped suddenly and fastened on your vitals. This is no mere figure of speech, but the true movement of experience. (187)

Austin identifies this presence as "Beauty-in-the-wild, yearning to be made human." It is a presence charged with a powerful eroti-

---

2. For a detailed discussion of this idea, see Snyder, *The Practice of the Wild*.

cism. The wild, Austin insists, is not found in books; it is something that escapes the "scholar." In an unpublished essay written in the 1920s, she elaborates on "Beauty-in-the-wild," emphasizing its erotic essence:

> It would come leaping out at me in odd contradictions of the accepted way of waking intelligence, with a keen sense of the long known, the reexperienced. . . . coyotes hot in the chase, and something older in me than thinking, off after them obsessed of the quarry, the entrancing, the utterly desired, sole object of endeavor, the delightful other of consummation. . . . O Delightful, I could eat you up. . . . I could love you to death! As I walked in the wild, now and then, with just such reversions of knowing and thinking, the animals "spoke" to me . . . and not animals only, plants . . . stones . . . mountains." ("Lost Others")

Austin is echoing a type of perception that D. H. Lawrence spent so much of his later years striving to express, particularly in the two cantankerous volumes *Psychoanalysis and the Unconscious* and *Fantasia of the Unconscious* (published later in a single edition). In the latter we find:

> There is a sensual way of beholding. There is the dark, desirous look of a savage who apprehends only that which has direct reference to himself, that which stirs a certain dark yearning within his lower self. Then his eye is fathomless blackness. But there is the dark eye which glances with a certain fire, and has no depth. There is a keen quick vision which watches, which beholds, but which never yields to the object outside: as a cat watching its prey. The dark glancing look which knows the *strangeness*, the danger of its object, the need to overcome the object. The eye which is not wide open to study, to learn, but which powerfully, proudly, or cautiously glances, and knows the terror or the pure desirability of strangeness in the object it beholds. The savage is all in all in himself. That which he sees outside he hardly notices or, sees as something odd, something automatically desirable, something lustfully desirable, or something dangerous. What we call vision, that he has not. (101)

Although they knew each other and Austin was familiar with Lawrence's work, she was not derivative—she had always experienced the world in this way.

Both writers were preoccupied with Eros. The erotic intensity of Austin's experience in San Fracisquito Canyon colors the language she uses to describe it, enlisting words normally reserved for recounting a lost or frustrated love affair of one's youth: "The occasion for giving herself up wholly to the mystery of the arroyos never arrived. And meantime, the place of the mystery was eaten up, it was made into building lots, cannery sites; it receded before the preëmptions of rock crushers and city dumps" (EH 187). Austin concludes this account: "Sometimes I think the frustration of that incomplete adventure is the source of the deep resentment I feel toward the totality of Southern California. It can't possibly be as inchoate and shallow as on its showing it appears, all the uses of natural beauty slavered over with the impudicity of a purely material culture. Other times, away from it, I wake in the night convinced that there are still uncorrupted corners from which the Spirit of the Arroyos calls me, wistful with long refusals, and I resolve that next year, or the *next* at farthest . . . and I am never able to manage it" (188). Two years after these words were published, their author was dead, apparently never having returned to the Arroyos. Desire in Austin's work is always predicated upon loss—lost borders, lost loves, lost lives.

Much of the Mary Austin we find in *Earth Horizon* is a consciously fashioned character who bears little resemblance to the historical Mary Austin known to family, friends, and acquaintances. Austin's most sympathetic biographer, Peggy Pond Church, has written: "All her life, the child named Mary would find it difficult to distinguish between dream and reality, between 'story-telling' and the truth of every day, between her father and mother as actual people and the characters she gave them in her own life's drama" (Church 45). For instance, when the narrator of *Earth Horizon* (a book whose voice vacillates between the first and third person) tells us that "there is something in Mary which comes out of the land," we might be inclined to take this as a figure of speech. However, Austin's intense perception of the presence of the wild is already manifest in her earliest surviving writings—the journals and notes she kept from 1888 to 1905, a record of what she later called "the pain of half forgotten passions" ("Lost Garden"), the karma of human experience lingering in the land itself.[3] We see this in *Lost Borders,* when she writes that "the reek of men's passion lies in the hollow desertness like an infection, as if every timber had absorbed mischief instead of moisture, and every bolt gives it off in lieu of rust" (CLB 167). She was determined to put into words "the impalpable somewhat that holds the record of human thought—of candles gone out—of fires burned down" (Graulich 217). Continuing on the theme of karma, she writes: "There is a belief among miners, very ill expressed or not expressed at all, that the hot essences of greed and hate and lust are absorbed, as it were, by the means that provoke them, and inhere in house, lands or stones to work mischief to the possessor." The land is haunted. When she writes about the wild, we should take her at her word.

In her unpublished "Tejon Notebook," twenty-year-old Mary Hunter writes this most intriguing entry:

> Coming down from Fort Tejon today I found a skull in the road with an ancient bullet hole. It had rolled down the hillside no doubt, but the strange thing was that I knew several minutes before I saw it what I was going to find, before I had turned the hill corner.
>
> Things like that happen to me here very often. There are times when everything seems to have a sinister kind of life. It shows its teeth at me. And at other times it is merely beautiful and gentle.
>
> Two or three times I have waked up in the night and had glimpses of what is sure to happen to me the next day. And there are times when I am called and called, I know just where the thing is which is calling, though I do not always know what. But as the call comes most often from places I have not been, mother will not let me go. I suppose it is not really safe, as I know so little about horses and people tell me it is easy to get lost. I heard Mother tell Mrs. Dunham that she hoped something would happen to give me a good scare, as she is never easy a minute when I am out of sight. I think the openness of everything scares mother, she has always lived in towns, and it frets her that I am not homesick. I can not make her understand that I am never homesick out of doors, but that in peoples houses, especially in houses that she calls "home-like" and "beautifully furnished"

---

3. "The Lost Garden." An unpublished essay written sometime prior to 1928, HEH catalog number AU 318. This quote comes in an earlier draft of the essay.

I am often very homesick. I used to be homesick in our own house. But I am not homesick with the sky, nor with the hills though sometime I am afraid of them.

Sometime the ruins at Fort Tejon try to tell me something, so that I feel hurt. I keep going from room to room to try and understand. There is a pink rose growing by one of them that is so homesick for its people that I could cry for it. (Austin Papers, HEH AU 267)

The wild "speaks" to her. Some might call this extrasensory perception, but for Austin this was a familiar mode of awareness. The land was trying to tell her something, something she was never quite able to grasp. (Later she would write that her trouble arose because "the country failed to explain itself" [EH 194]). The land is beautiful, but it is also "sinister"—it bares its "teeth"—a figure she resorts to several times in her later writings. She recognizes that there is a significant part of the wild that *should* be feared. In this sense, she prefigures the poetry of Robert Frost.

Finally, interwoven with this account of the wild is Austin's tempestuous relationship with her mother—the two relationships would always intertwine. This conflation of the wild and mother provides the brooding core of Austin's essay on the Sierra Madre, or "Mothering Mountains," in *California, Land of the Sun*: "The orange orchards lay dead green in the hollows, unplanted ridges showed scarcely a trace of atmospheric blueness; unlaced, unbuskined, the land rested. And all in the falling of a leaf, in the scuttle of a horned toad in the dust of the roadway, it lifted into eerie life. It bared its teeth; the veil of the mountains was rent. Nothing changed, nothing stirred or glimmered, but the land had spoken. As if it had taken a step forward, as if a hand were raised, the mountain stood over us. And then it sank again. While the chill was still on us, the grip of terror, there lay the easy land, the comfortable crops, the red geraniums about the bungalows. But never again for me would the Sierra Madre be a mere geographical item, a feature of the landscape; it was Power, immanent and inescapable. Shall not the mother of the land do what she will with it?" (39).

The act of writing, for Austin as for many others, provided release. Her relationship with her mother remained a source of great psychological strain, one that she couldn't address directly until later in life, well after Susie Hunter's death. In the meantime, the undischarged energy swirling about in Austin's psyche over her problems with her mother was rechanneled into a heightened perception of the land, and later her problems were intensified further by the failure of her marriage and the apparent mental disability of her only child, a daughter. Through these long years, Austin wrote down her "impressions" of the wild, later composing them into writings that she would publish. Some of these early handwritten notes survive, and appended to them is a typewritten memo dated July 24, 1917:

> There were such quantities of the words, facts, fortunate phrases jotted down on any scrap of paper that came to hand. It was a relief to the poignancy with which every thing in nature affected me. I was too much alive to these things, almost a part of the[m], I suffered. Nobody around me cared in the least.
>
> I wrote them down and after I had written a book I used to go through my notes and destroy everything I had used in the book. Even with that precaution I used to repeat. . . . It took me years to let the thing go out of my mind, the picture[,] the poignant perception. It was always necessary to my happiness to do something with these gleanings of the wild. After I had found just the right use for a descriptive phrase, the final absolute use of it would leave me. I kept too much, was always indanger [*sic*] of using too much, putting too many good phrases into my book, not because they were good phrase[s] but because they were living perceptions that tormented me. I had to get my house in order. I am crowded, stiffled [*sic*] always with pictures. I know too much and not well enough. Fortunately those phrases of the Wild have been snowed under by later phrases of sophistication. These are mere reminders[;] drift of a flood. As such they may interest somebody. (Stineman 34)

In its tone, this typescript is typically Austin. Her perceptions of the wild "tormented" her, but nobody "cared in the least." She was always, at least from her perspective, an "outsider." This posture creates a significant problem for even a sympathetic reader of Austin's work: one gets the impression that, while the writer is giving an accurate account of her experience, she is compelled to deliver it with a stridency suggesting that *she* was the only one privy to such experience. In matters of creativity and "genius"—one of her favorite subjects in later work—Mary Austin believed in an "aristocracy of the spirit." Inevitably, she approaches her reader from a position of beleaguered loftiness. In a 1925 letter to Mabel Dodge Luhan, Austin writes: "My early life made me stiff to know. . . . [I have] a deep seated resistance to being personally liked. Nothing stiffens me quite so much as being called 'charming'" (Stineman 158). Even in her personal letters, she never achieves an intimate voice.

Nevertheless, her perceptions of the wild are of interest—especially for the *method* she used to gather them, which amounts to a practiced "watching." Responding to her publisher's request for a biographical sketch and an account of the genesis of *The Land of Little Rain*, Austin wrote:

> I can't do it . . . I thought it would be easy to do, but it isn't. There is really nothing to tell. I have just looked, nothing more, when I was too sick to do anything else, I could lie out under the sage brush and look, and when I was able to get about I went to look at other things, and by and by I got to know when and where looking was most worthwhile..Then I got so full of looking I had to write to get rid of some of it to make room for more. (Fink 110)

In *Earth Horizon*, she claims: "Only the Christian saints have made the right words for it, and to them it came after long discipline of renunciation. But to Mary it just happened. Ultimate, immaterial reality" (198). Austin's work can be read as an extension of the American tradition of Transcendental Mediumship, which has been defined as a "subtle fusion of nature worship and occult sensitivity." For nineteenth-century American women—Emily Dickinson among them—such spiritualism provided "an outlet for their stifled sensitivity and longing for acclaim" (St. Armand 7, 18). We must keep in mind, however, that more than simply a "tradition," Austin's life and work attest to a way of being in the world, an existential method that has remarkable affinities with the Taoist notion of *wu-wei*, which translates as "without-action" or "inaction." *Wu-wei*, as Burton Watson explains it, is "not a forced quietude, but a course of action that is not founded upon any purposeful motives of gain or striving. In such a state, all human actions become as spontaneous and mindless as those of the natural world."[4] Austin's method might also be called Buddhist. As Alan Watts explains:

> For Buddhism . . . is not a system of doctrines or commandments re-quiring belief and obedience. It is a method (one of the exact mean-ings of dharma) for the correction of our perceptions and for the transformation of consciousness. It is so thoroughly experimental and empirical that the actual subject-matter of Buddhism must be said to be immediate, non-verbal experience rather than a set of beliefs or ideas or rules of behavior.
>
> In sum, Buddhism is a method for changing one's sense of identity, that is, of the way in which one experiences the fact of being alive.[5]

Austin's method of watching the wild led her to the conclusion that the subject/object dichotomy so often insisted upon in main-stream American culture is, in reality, a form of *mis*-perception.

In the Huntington Library's collection, there are some notes on old paper, probably dating from Austin's years in the Owens Valley. These scraps reveal the radical sweep of her perception:

> What I see in nature is mind[,] conscious mind reacting on mind shaping the world. Mind in the trees and birds and insects, mind in flowers. That is how they come to resemble one another. The mind of the bird asks a question of the insect, Are you good to eat? The ef-fort of the insect is to answer no, to tell a fib[,] to seem to be not good to eat
>
> I feel this interchange. There is communication between all living things. Once I lost it and the tree was only a vegetable growth to me and the world was a strange cold place[,] very lonely. I feel this com-munication physically, between my shoulders in the back of the neck. I feel it physically after sitting a long time silent. I almost understand what it says. Indians tell me of remarkable instances when they have known the thoughts of animals by this means. I am sure that it is pos-sible. (Austin Papers, HEH AU 363)

A similar description of her somatic response to the wild unfolds in "The Friend in the Wood": "Let who will walk in the wild long enough to lose the feel of conventional securities and he will begin to go stilly, with vague apprisals of unease along the back of the

---

4. Burton Watson, trans., *Chuang Tzu* (6). The term *wu* ("nothing") is some-times used for the *tao*.

5. Prefatory essay to D. T. Suzuki, *Outlines of Mahayana Buddhism* (xi).

neck and between the shoulders, to sleep with an unspecified sense awake, and all the others, hearing, sight, and smell—raised to forgotten levels of sensitivity. As if in every cell of man there is a latent life of knowingness left over from whatever animal ancestor contributed it" (Church 187).

When we realize Austin's method of perception, her practice of the wild, we are better able to understand her when, at the end of her life, she writes that "[t]here is something in Mary which comes out of the land; something in its rhythms, its living compulsions." Furthermore, we can see that her method and her perception are at odds with what she calls "the male ritual of rationalization" (EH 15). The object of her scorn is the same as John Muir's: science as it was taught in the American universities; science as it was practiced by Clarence King, the Whitney Survey, and the U.S. Geological Survey; science as it was executed by engineers and condoned by U.S. government policy that eventually culminated in the huge water-reclamation projects that erupted across the arid West during the course of Austin's own lifetime.

Austin's method of perception, like Muir's, was predicated upon intuition. She did not have a scientifically convincing data base to use in her explanations. When she voiced her opinions in the world of science or politics, she was not taken seriously—certainly not as seriously as she wished to be taken—because she was a woman, because she was a poet, because she was prone to "mysticism." Austin's work flows in a stream of women's writing that has its source in the middle of the nineteenth century, in a tradition of *identification with* nature that runs counter to that which would *control* it. "Indeed," Paula Bennett writes, "what is most striking about American women's statements on nature in this period is the degree to which these writers were prepared to trust nature and to identify with her" (92). To the end of her life, Austin never doubted the validity of her own experience, what she learned from the wild, but, if we are to judge from the tone of her autobiography, she seldom found a sympathetic audience, even among those who "appreciated" nature writing:

> And still, whenever, out of a car window, over the wall of a rich man's garden, about which I am being proudly shown by the proprietor, I get sight of any not utterly ruined corner of it, I am torn in my

vitals. This is the way a Naturist is taken with the land, with the spirit trying to be evoked out of it. This is the authentic note of confession for which autobiographies are supposed to be written, for which they are quite certainly read. It is time somebody gave a true report. All the public expects of the experience of practicing Naturists is the appearance, the habits, the incidents of the wild; when the Naturist reports upon himself, it is mistaken for poetizing. (EH 188)

Even Austin's mother, if we are to believe the tale, attempted to thwart her daughter's interest in nature (not to mention sex):

Moreover, Susie had taken pains to impress upon [Mary] the childish character of her interest in nature and the inexpedience of talking about it. Especially you must not talk appreciatively about landscapes and flowers and the habits of little animals and birds to boys; they didn't like it. If one of them took you walking, your interest should be in your companion, and not exceed a ladylike appreciation of the surroundings, in so far as the boy, as the author of the walk, might feel himself complimented by your appreciation of it. You must not quote; especially poetry and Thoreau. An occasional reference to Burroughs was permissible, but not Thoreau. A very little experience demonstrated that Susie was right. You gathered that outdoors as a subject of conversation was boring to most people. (112)

One gathers from this passage just how much erotic energy was invested—or should we say "sublimated"—into the natural world by nineteenth-century American culture. The walk itself was a vehicle for Eros. It brings to mind John Muir's walks with Emily Pelton in Wisconsin—not to mention his ten years of erotic rambling in the Sierra Nevada.

In fact, one of the few people Mary Austin met who did sympathize with her perceptions of the wild was John Muir himself, whom she described as "a tall, lean man with the habit of talking much, the habit of soliloquizing. He told stories of his life in the wild, and of angels; angels that saved him; that lifted and carried him; that showed him where to put his feet; he believed them. I told him one of mine; except that I didn't see mine. I had been lifted and carried; I had been carried out of the way of danger; and he believed me" (298). Austin admits that she didn't identify too strongly with Muir's way of personifying the wild because she found "the pietistic characteristics of angels" too reminiscent of the brand of Christianity she was raised with, the sort of institutionalized religion she rejected most vehemently. Yet she was in tune with the wild throes of Eros that Muir's lingering Calvinism repressed in him. When Muir "saw" the wild he saw disembodied angels. Austin, on the other hand, perceived the wild not as angel, but as woman.

Immediately following her mention of Muir in *Earth Horizon*, she presents the anecdote of a man whose story "illustrate[d] what she [herself] felt in the desert wild." She calls it the story of "the One Woman":

> He had met her when he was young and obsessed with the Life adventure. He knew her for what she was to be to him, and refused to know; there were so many other charming women in the world; he didn't want to be taken with the net of permanence so early; he could come back to her when he had tried and preferred. And he was never able to get back. That was a long time ago, he said, and there were still times when he would be seized with the certainty of the One Woman, the dreadful, never-to-be-appeased desire of her. (188)

Austin correlates this One Woman with her own Spirit of the Arroyos, whom she had encountered in San Francisquito Canyon. Both figures hum with thwarted desire. "She meant to come back to wrestle with the Spirit of the Arroyos, and she was never able. One quiet year to get a modern return on a persisting type of human experience on which even the intelligent Greeks spent themselves . . . not obtainable in the wealthiest country in the world!" Whereas the wild, in the form of the One Woman, is bodied forth as a lost lover for the man (such as John Muir), the wild for Mary Austin becomes a feminine spirit that must be "wrestled." The wild is no lover; rather, it is a powerful force—not unlike, as Austin makes quite clear, a domineering mother—that must be confronted.

Austin never failed to personify the wild as female. "If the desert were a woman," she writes in the first chapter of *Lost Borders*, "I know well what like she would be: deep-breasted, broad in the hips, tawny hair, great masses of it lying smooth along her perfect curves, full lipped like a sphinx, but not heavy-lidded like one, eyes sane and steady as the polished jewel of her skies, such a countenance as should make men serve without desiring her, such a largeness to her mind as should make their sins of no account, passionate, but not necessitous, patient—and you could not move her, no, not if you had all the earth to give, so much as one tawny hair's-breadth beyond her own desires" (CLB 160). In *California, Land of the Sun,* she says that "a great land, like a great lady, has her way with men" (10). And in *Earth Horizon,* she imparts to her reader "the searing knowledge of the ways of the land with men . . . a spell of its lofty and intricate charm, which worked on men like the beauty of women" (270). Austin draws a sharp distinction between men and women in the effect that the same land has on them. Whereas men "felt themselves enchanted [by the desert], [w]ith the women it was not so; they felt, as they hung there suspended between hopes that refused to eventuate, life slipping away from them" (285). *The Land of Little Rain* and, especially, *Lost Borders* document the infidelities of males, males seduced by the wild, and the ramifications of these seductions on the women who depend upon the males. Women in these stories have not come to the desert by choice. Austin suggests that the wild is a rival feminine force with which women must first contend but then ultimately be reconciled. Men, too, must come to terms with this feminine force, but the ways in which they can accomplish this are different. Ultimately, according to Austin, reconciliation between the human and the wild can only be achieved through reconciliation between women and men, through the founding of an egalitarian social order.

## A Loss of Borders

Men were attracted to the desert for its gold, but the overriding theme of *The Land of Little Rain* is that none exists save for the alchemical gold. The successful miner is the one who unearths the philosopher's stone. The desert always takes from those who expect it to give—and the desert is always bigger than they think. "Nothing so large as a man can move unspied upon in that country, and [the vultures] know well how the land deals with strangers.

There are hints to be had here of the way in which a land forces new habits on its dwellers" (CLB 15). In the overwhelming emptiness, something does emerge from nothing: Mystery. *The Land of Little Rain* is its author's testament to the fact that the word *desert* is etymologically related to *sorcery*: "The palpable sense of mystery in the desert air breeds fables, chiefly of lost treasure" (16). For Mary Austin, the alchemical gold is refined by telling a story.

Although Austin is regarded as a premier "naturist" in the tradition of Thoreau, Muir, and King, more importantly she should be known as a storyteller. All her stories and sketches in *The Land of Little Rain* and *Lost Borders* bear the mark of autobiography; she blurs the distinction, the border, between fiction and nonfiction. "Mary lived in her writing," Mabel Dodge Luhan wrote of her friend, "which was entirely autobiographic even when she wrote of river and deserts. She always identified herself with her subject" (Houghland 20). Since *The Land of Little Rain* and *Lost Borders* emerge from the same source—Austin's years in the Owens Valley of California—the two books can easily be read as one extended work.[6] Whereas the former focuses on the land itself and sets the scene, the latter delineates the land's effect upon human character, upon the individuals who come to live in the desert.

Austin's "Country of Lost Borders" has a geography of liminality. She insists that the native Shoshones and Paiutes recognized this psychological dimension of the Mojave Desert, adapting themselves and their culture to it, but the white man has much to learn—or *un*-learn—about it:

> The boundaries between the tribes and between the clans within the tribes were plainly established by natural landmarks—peaks, hillcrests, creeks, and chains of water-holes—beginning at the foot of the Sierra and continuing eastward past the limit of endurable existence. Out there, a week's journey from everywhere, the land was not worth parcelling off, and the boundaries which should logically have been continued until they met the cañon of the Colorado ran out in foolish wastes of sand and inextricable disordered ranges. Here you have the significance of the Indian name for that country—Lost Borders. (CLB 155)

---

6. Thus, Rutgers University Press publishes the two works in one edition.

The loss of geographical borders parallels a loss of psychological borders: the wild threatens law, conscience, and, indeed, ego with dissolution. "Clear out beyond the Borders," she writes, "the only unforgivable offense is incompetence; and conscience, in as far as it is a hereditary prejudice in favor of a given line of behavior, is not the sort of baggage to take into the wilderness, which has its own exigencies and occasions, and will not be lived in except upon its own conditions" (167). The desert destroys those who are not prepared to change the way they live their lives, but it always offers the possibility of self-transformation:

> Great souls that go into the desert come out mystics—saints and prophets—declaring unutterable things: Buddha, Mahomet, and the Galilean, convincing of the casual nature of human relations, because the desert itself has no use for the formal side of man's affairs. What need, then, of so much pawing over precedent and discoursing upon it, when the open country lies there, a sort of chemist's cup for resolving obligations? Say whether, when all decoration is eaten away, there remains any bond and what you shall do about it. (180)

Voluntarily (as with saints) or involuntarily (as with most of the white men in Austin's sketches), the self will be unselfed.

After first informing her reader in *Lost Borders* that the "law runs with the boundary, not beyond it," Austin's narrator goes on to say: "I am convinced that most men make law for the comfortable feel of it, defining them to themselves; they shoulder along like blindworms. . . . They pinch themselves with regulations to make sure of being sentient, and organize within organizations." As a reluctant—and indeed *involuntary*—pilgrim to the wild, Mary Austin took refuge in observing and recording the spectacle of white men and women confronting the desert:

> Out there, then, where the law and the landmarks fail together, the souls of little men fade out at the edges, leak from them as water from wooden pails warped asunder.
>
> Out there where the borders of conscience break down, where there is no convention, and behavior is of little account except as it gets you your desire, almost anything might happen; does happen, in fact, though I shall have trouble making you believe it. Out there where the boundary of soul and sense is as faint as a trail in a sandstorm, I have seen things happen that I do not believe myself. (156)

The dissolution of borders is a sort of mobile anti-structure, anti-hierarchy, as Deleuze and Guattari phrase it. It opens up that dangerous creative SPACE (in Charles Olson's sense of the word) wherein the self, including its possibilities for reimagining its idea of community, is reformulated. Here, the self is made anew—or obliterated entirely. Here is where Clarence King and Everett Ruess disappeared. Here is where Henry Thoreau and John Muir acquired their social vision. Here is where Mary Austin began to write and discover what she called the American Rhythm. "For all the desert takes of a man it gives compensations, deep breaths, deep sleep, and the communion of the stars" (17).

The desert takes a tremendous toll on unprepared human beings. In an unpublished essay, Austin writes that "the last, most irreparable of the assaults the desert makes on man is to rob him of the imaginations of his heart. I have seen men who have lived much in lonely places, flattened out, shrunk to the dimensions of a husk by the loss of the power of dreaming" ("Lost Garden"). This, indeed, is the relentless theme of all her stories from the Country of Lost Borders. Representative in this regard is "The Return of Mr. Wills," the opening paragraph of which telegraphs the entire plot:

> Mrs. Wills had lived seventeen years with Mr. Wills, and when he left her for three, those were so much the best of her married life that she wished he had never come back. And the only real trouble with Mr. Wills was that he should never have moved West. Back East I suppose they breed such men because they need them, but they ought really to keep them there. (CLB 181)

Mr. Wills was the "sort of man bred up in close communities, like a cask, to whom the church, public opinion, the social note, are a sort of hoop to hold him in serviceable shape. Without these there are a good many ways of going to pieces." He went to pieces because he "was troubled with an imagination" of a lost mine. Mr. Wills, like so many people, was troubled by unslaked desire—and he directed it toward a chimera. Little did he realize the wild power of this chimera. "Out there beyond the the towns the long Wilderness lies brooding, imperturbable; she puts out to adventurous minds glittering fragments of fortune or romance, like the lures

men use to catch antelopes—clip! then she has them." Mr. Wills
was seduced. He pursued the lost mine, which, Austin emphati-
cally reports, was actually a pursuit of the wild itself. For all his efforts, he simply disappeared one day. "The fact was, the desert had
got him. All the hoops were off the cask. The mind of Mr. Wills
faded out at the edges like the desert horizon that melts in mists
and mirages, and finally he went on an expedition from which he
did not come back" (184).

The theme of this story, however, is not the seduction of Mr.
Wills, but the liberation—albeit temporary—of Mrs. Wills. After
her husband had disappeared, she went to work for herself and became quite successful. She discovered that "she not only did not
need Mr. Wills, but got on better without him." Unfortunately, he
returned after three years—upon hearing that his son had been injured—and Mr. Wills once again "settled on his family like a
blight." The desert had "sucked the life out of him and cast him
back." Austin depicts him as the unfaithful husband, rejected by
his illicit lover (that is, the desert), come home at last for lack of
anywhere else to go. His affections, though, remain elsewhere, for
"he had brought the desert with him on his back . . . [a]nd the
power of the wilderness lay like a wasting sickness on the home."
Mrs. Wills should have divorced her husband, but "the church to
which [she] belonged admitted divorce only in the event of there
being another woman." Unfortunately, "[t]he minister himself was
newly from the East, and did not understand that the desert is to
be dealt with as a woman and a wanton; he was thinking of it as a
place on the map." Austin concludes her ironic tale with Mrs.
Wills, "her gaze wandering to the inscrutable grim spaces, not with
the hate you might suppose, but with something like hope in her
eye, as if she had guessed what I am certain of—that in time its insatiable spirit will reach out and take Mr. Wills again."

As happens in many of the sketches in *The Land of Little Rain*
and *Lost Borders*, a man is seduced by the wild and then brought
into submission, whereas the woman who depends upon him is left
to fend for herself. Inevitably, the woman emerges as the stronger
character, for she is the one who recognizes that "[n]ot the law but
the land sets the limit" (CLB 9). Mr. Wills, on the other hand, is
typical of the men Austin knew in the Mojave Desert. "Mind you,"

she writes, "it is men who go mostly into the desert, who love it past all reasonableness, slack their ambitions, cast off old usages, neglect their families because of the pulse and beat of a life laid bare to its thews and sinews. Their women hate with implicitness the life like the land, stretching interminably whity-brown, dim and shadowy blue hills that hem it, glimmering pale waters of mirage that creep and crawl about its edges" (159–60). At first, the women hate "the vast impersonal rivalry of desertness" (175) because they did not choose to come to this place; they came because their men brought them here. But while the men are out chasing mirages, the women slowly come to terms with the desert, coming to know it, respect it, and finally learn from it.

Austin's most powerful expression of women's potential for establishing mutual relation—both to the wild *and* to men—is her sketch in *Lost Borders* entitled "The Walking Woman." The main character here is a nomad, a liminar, a woman who circumambulates the borderlands of civilization. She is at the fringe of nominalization as well: "She was the Walking Woman, and no one knew her name. . . . She came and went about our western world on no discoverable errand. . . . She came and went, oftenest on a kind of muse of travel which the untrammeled space begets, or at rare intervals flooding wondrously with talk, never of herself, but of things she had known or seen" (CLB 255). A woman to match John Muir: walker, watcher, and storyteller.

The Walking Woman began her nomadic life by "walking off an illness." Austin's narrator tells us that "it may very well have been an unsoundness of mind which drove her to the open, sobered and healed at last by the large soundness of nature," what Gretel Ehrlich has called the solace of open spaces. "It must have been then that she lost her name" (CLB 257). The Walking Woman presents a striking contrast to the other desert nomads, all of whom are male, since she is not looking for a lost mine, nor is she hoping to stake a claim or pursuing any chimera. She simply walks, and in so doing she leaves behind the social conventions that otherwise keep women "in their place." "She had walked off all sense of society-made values, and, knowing the best when the best came to her, was able to take it" (261).

The bundle of society-made values that the Walking Woman

most forcefully rejects is the Cult of True Womanhood. "I worked with a man," she tells the narrator, "without excusing, without any burden on me of looking or seeming. Not fiddling or fumbling as women work, and hoping it will all turn out for the best" (259). For the Walking Woman—as for Austin—love between human beings does not emerge from "looking and seeming" but from working together: "To work together, to love together" (261). The Walking Woman echoes Austin's own values in this regard. In *Earth Horizon* she writes that "the true ground of intimacy between men and women is their common fixation on an undescribed Third—a Way of Life, a child, a common attack upon the Wilderness" (174). In her own life, Austin blamed the failure of her marriage on the fact that she and her husband, Stafford, never established mutuality, never triangulated on the "undescribed Third." She staunchly placed the responsibility for failure on Stafford, who was "so deeply and intimately committed to his own way of life" that he neglected to consider that Mary had needs of her own. Austin complains of "the total want of coördination in the most venerable fidelities of marriage, the common fronting of man and woman to the wilderness" (CLB 243).[7] "The Walking Woman," with its celebration of a female whose own "doing" displaces the society-made "looking and seeming," reads as a projection of its author's ideal self.

Over the course of her lifework, Austin directs her reader's attention to "that which the world knows so little what to do with that it mostly throws it away—a good woman with great power and possibilities of passion" (206). Her own life in the Owens Valley was characterized by "hardship and domestic woe, which she later described as 'long dull months of living interspersed with the few fruitful occasions when I actually came into contact with the Land'" (Fink 79). During the 1890s, Austin became painfully aware of the failure of the three most important relationships of

---

7. Austin is the only one of the writers I have been considering who broaches the subject of sex. In an essay entitled "Sex in American Literature," she writes: "[T]he whole institution of marriage is built up out of this subconscious conviction of women that the common life of husband and wife, what they may achieve by way of offspring, by conquest of the maternal environment, or on the plane of perceptive consciousness, is more important than what they feel for one another."

her life: those with her mother, husband, and daughter. She was terribly lonely, often in poor health. In "How I Learned to Read and Write" (reprinted in Hart), she says that she composed *The Land of Little Rain* following a serious illness: "I was languid with convalescence, I was lonely; and quite suddenly I began to write." In *Earth Horizon*, she tells us that "the thing Mary suffered from in the middle nineties was loneness; by which I mean to indicate a state of lacking human resort, rather than any emotional state which involved feeling sorry for herself" (268). Traces of this pain course throughout the fictional territory of the Country of Lost Borders. The predominant theme of Austin's lifework is ultimately loss.

The failure of her relationships with mother, daughter, and husband are important touchstones in understanding Austin's relationship to the wild. Her mother died in 1896, before the two were able to achieve any sort of reconciliation. Susie Hunter and Mary Austin never understood one another as individual human beings. Although never able to forgive her mother on a personal level, Austin did come to a sort of archetypal understanding of "the Mother," made possible only in the dissolution of borders that death brings for the individual ego. Of her mother's death Austin writes:

> There is an element of incalculable ravening in the loss of your mother; deep under the shock of broken habit and the ache of present grief, there is the psychic wound, the severed root of being; such loss as makes itself felt as the companion of immortality. For how should the branch suffer, torn from the dead tree? It is only when the tree is green that the cut bough bleeds. (EH 273)

Here, Austin confronted an psychological emptiness as vast as the desert itself—the lost territory of a mother–daughter relationship.

The pain of Austin's failure as daughter was mirrored and amplified by her own failure at motherhood. Ruth Austin was born in 1892, and it quickly became apparent that there was something wrong with the child. Although the actual nature of her affliction is not clear, Ruth suffered some form of mental disability. (Austin blamed Ruth's problems on a genetic defect inherited from Stafford Austin's side of the family.) In any case, despite her later claims that she intensely desired to have children, it would seem that Austin was not entirely committed to the prospect, or she may simply have been unprepared for all that motherhood entails.[8] In 1900, Austin placed Ruth with a family to take care of her; later, she put her into a private institution in Santa Clara, California, where Ruth died in a flu epidemic in 1914. Years later, in writing about her own experience of motherhood, Austin recalls once again her own mother. Here we see a link between desire, motherhood, loss, and creativity:

> In a way this tragic end of my most feminine adventure brought the fulfillment of my creative desire, which had begun to be an added torment by repression. Caring for a hopelessly invalid child is an expensive business. I had to write to make money. In the end I was compelled to put my child in a private institution where she was happier and better cared for than I could otherwise manage. . . . To my own family [that is, her mother] who demanded somewhat accusingly what they should say, I said: "You can say I have lost her." Which was true and a great relief to them. My mother died shortly after, but was never quite reconciled to my refusal to accept my trouble as a clear sign of God's displeasure. ("Woman Alone" 229)

Daughter, like mother, had been "lost." The desire that might have been channeled into these relationships was redirected into the production of writing.

In regard to Thoreau, Barbara Johnson asks: "How might the plot of human subjectivity be reconceived (so to speak) if pregnancy rather than autonomy is what raises the question of deliberateness?" (190). This question is particularly applicable to Mary Austin, as it calls attention to the human body itself, its wildness. The issue of motherhood, with its complex assortment of biological and cultural questions, is one of the "wildest" that may be raised. The male writers I have been considering eschew the subject, despite all their acknowledgment of nature's "feminine" com-

---

8. Austin was highly regarded as a cook, but suffered great criticism for the way she treated her daughter. Late in life, and probably in answer to some of the criticism she had received, she writes: "Contrary to the popular conception about literary women, I like domestic life and have a genuine flair for cooking. And I wanted children profoundly." See "Woman Alone" (229).

ponent—for them, motherhood is simply not an issue. For Austin, however, it is the central issue. Continually confronting what Julia Kristeva refers to as the paradox of the mother, Austin's writings on motherhood can be understood in the context of an elaborated narcissism. Kristeva writes:

> If it is not possible to say of a *woman* what she *is* (without running the risk of abolishing her difference), would it perhaps be different concerning the *mother*, since that is the only function of the "other sex" to which we can definitely attribute existence? And yet, there too, we are caught in a paradox. First, we live in a civilization where the *consecrated* (religious or secular) representation of femininity is absorbed by motherhood. If, however, one looks at it more closely, this motherhood is the fantasy that is nurtured by the adult, man or woman, of a lost territory; what is more, it involves less an idealized archaic mother than the idealization of a *relationship* that binds us to her, one that cannot be localized—an idealization of primary narcissism. (*Kristeva Reader* 161)

The "fantasy" (or ideal image) of motherhood is derived from cultural sources; it is another social institution—the very thing Austin would resist.

Nevertheless, she clearly recognizes the "wild" element in motherhood—a revelation that comes to her, if we are to believe her account, when she was overwhelmed for the first time in her life by blind fear. She recounts this most fantastic incident in an essay she herself never published, entitled "The Friend in the Wood":

> There were three of us making camp in one of the desert cañons of the east sloping Sierras. There it became necessary for me to be left alone with my baby for practically the whole of one day; not in itself an occasion of terror. No objective danger was to be feared, nor was there anything in my experience to suggest any other terror. Uneasiness began about mid-morning with the growing sense of personality in grey ribbed hills and the rushing water under the cottonwoods. Slowly at first, and then menacingly, the mountains came alive, they swelled with unappeasable insistence that filled the cañon like a tide. I fought the onslaught for a while, with wave on wave of succumbing in which the one strange point of sanity was the baby, cooing and unaware. It was *my* fear, my inescapable piled up terror, before which

presently I dropped my gun—for this was no instinctive animal warn-
ing of avoidable danger, such as I had had, times enough, in the
open—and tying my baby around my neck, as I suppose my fore-
mothers had done in the grip of original fright, I climbed into a size-
able tree. I was only twenty-two, and I had never known fear before;
and what can one do when the friendly earth denies you! I remember
tying the baby's blanket, hammock-wise, safely into the horizontal
boughs, as though it were the last thing I was to do, and giving myself
up to being overwhelmingly sick with the sickness of a house-bred
dog when it comes unexpectedly upon the spoor of a wolf. From
where I clung in the middle branches of my tree, I could see no sky,
and was partly screened by leafage from the menace of the naked
mountain walls; so as I pressed against the trunk of the tree and made
with my body a little answering warmth, assurance began to creep up
to me with the sap. I was able at last to bring my will to bear on the
threatening wild, to compel it back to its normal state of earth and
stone again. I did not know then what the Indians afterward taught
me, of the measures for exorcising this most ancient terror of the
Earth-will, but by degrees, measured by sharp recurrences of paralyz-
ing fright, I felt the earth spell subside. Presently resentment came to
reinforce such courage as I had,—for how can one know much of
courage, either who has been unfamiliar with fear—the resentment of
the Sacred Middle against the insubordinate earth it is predestined to
subdue. (Church 191–92)

Among the more remarkable things to emerge from this most remarkable passage is Austin's idea of a human femininity opposed
to the "insubordinate earth," a femininity that—allied with what
she calls the "Sacred Middle" (purportedly an Indian notion)—ex-
erts a will to power over primordial chaos. If nothing else, this passage sheds some light on a claim she makes in *Lost Borders*, that
"mostly in encounter with the primal forces woman gets the worst
of it except now and then, when there are children in question,
she becomes a primal force herself" (CLB 180).

    Austin's story suggests the reenactment of a feminine creation
myth.[9] The tree she climbed and clung to mediates between the
human (what she sometimes calls the "man-mind") and the

---

9. We might, however, question the "fact" of her story here. She claims to
have been twenty-two years old at the time, but she did not have Ruth until she
was twenty-four.

"threatening wild": "as I pressed against the trunk of the tree and made with my body a little answering warmth, assurance began to creep up to me with the sap." Recalling that the ancient druids not only practiced "tree-magic" but used trees as an alphabet in their divination practices, we can read Austin's "creation" myth of the Sacred Middle versus the Threatening Wild as a myth that explores the origins of language itself.[10] The tree functions as a concrete intermediary of the Sacred Middle, which is itself—as we will see—an emptiness or nonlocalized space. This emptiness, this space without borders—what Kristeva (borrowing her terminology from Plato) calls the *chora*—is the provenance of rhythm. And it was rhythm that preoccupied Austin in her later years.

### The Rhythmic Stream

Mary Austin's most intriguing yet perplexing book is *The American Rhythm*. It saw two editions, one in 1923 and a revised, expanded version in 1930. On the one hand, it is her magnum opus; on the other, it is hopelessly obscure; and herein lies its unfathomable beauty. The investigation of rhythm and its origins—particularly in its effect upon American culture—dominated her intellectual interests over the last fifteen years of her life.

There is always something cosmological in Austin's writings about rhythm. Her most poetic—and perhaps most accessible—expression of the importance that rhythm played in her own creative life occurs in a letter to her botanist friend Daniel Trembly MacDougal:

> I like to dive into a rhythmic stream like a fish into the gulf current and go where it takes me. I like to be a sun swinging through space with all my seven planets disposed about me, and I like to be the green flush that creeps up and dies rhythmically along the side of Palo Corona. Best of all, I like to flash into the life rhythm of some other human being, and find myself suddenly knowing all about what

---

10. See Robert Graves, *The White Goddess*; in particular, chapters 10 and 11 concerning "The Tree-Alphabet." Graves regards the tree-alphabet "as genuine relic of Druidism orally transmitted down the centuries" (165).

it was, now and will be. Then I like to repeat some of these experiences by writing books or poems about them. (Stineman 127)

Austin's words here are reminiscent of the windy discussion of the "One" in that most inexplicable of the Platonic dialogues, the *Parmenides*: "Now, since the one is in time and has the property of becoming older and younger, it has a past, a future, and a present. Consequently the one was and is and will be, and it was becoming, and will become. Also, it can be said to *have* something, and there can be something *of* it, alike in past, present, and future. So there can be knowledge and opinion and perception of it" (155d). Austin's "perception" of the One, we could say, is conducted via rhythm. The stream of rhythm is a stream of desire—its flows circulate in boundless space, the unutterable motion behind all words.

Kristeva identifies desire, "stripped down to its basic structure," as rhythm itself, "the conjunction of body and music" (*Kristeva Reader* 295). Rhythm is prelinguistic in its origins, thus "wild," and it presents a formidable problem to the literary artist. The goal—or sometimes, the accident—of any literary pilgrimage to the wild is to "get beyond" the words, but then to return with a story. This is a major insight, one that Austin never wearied of presenting to her readers—it is the revelation of her practice of the wild: "the illuminations which came from those silent sessions in the wild were of the sort which set in motion the search for words, for nice distinctions of definition, for intricate unfoldings of smooth-pointed buds of suggestion" ("Friend in the Wood," in Church 195). It was necessary for Austin to find the Country of Lost Borders, where "[n]ot the law but the land sets the limit," because it was the site of her creativity, where she did not have to contend with all the social restrictions, especially those that applied to women. "The poetic," Kristeva tells us, "would be that which has not become law." The poetic is but another name for the wild.

And what of beauty? And sexual desire? Austin links these most slippery terms into her formulation of the wild when she refers to "a presence natural to the outdoors," which she claims is easily intuited by children. In "The Friend in the Wood," she explains how, when she was a child, she and her female friends were fully aware of this feeling, that it was identified with appreciations of beauty: beauty of the wild, of moonlit groves and budding gardens, with the hot color of the maples in October. . . . And by degrees it passed for the others—but never for me—into a nameless urge that demanded presence for fulfillment . . . [which] left an image of emptiness, never in my case to be filled by blurred presentiments of "a boy I know."

I think I must have gone through a period of pretense that for me, also, beauty in the wild was the mysterious foreshadowing of the mate as it was for my companions. It would have been so natural a way for the mate to come, all the way out of childhood, foreknown as Beauty and so certified to be the absolute One. . . . But for me beauty in the wild took no appeasement from the mate. Never at all the mate!

With a puzzled sense of desertion I saw the Presence withdraw itself from my companions, saw the wild empty itself for them to the mere dimension of line and color and association. . . . Americans generally, though they wish it known that they approve of fine landscape, do not care for discussions of it, or of beauty as an item by itself. Women, I suspect, withdraw themselves from the appeal of the Wild because it distracts them from that compacted rounding of themselves which is indispensable to the feminine achievement. (Church 186–87)

Austin has formulated here an etiology of desire that rivals those of Plato and Freud: desire for a "mate" is the result of a "withdrawal" of the "beauty in the wild." This is not Freudian repression or even sublimation, but simply an "emptying," what Kristeva would call "abjection," that is, desire deprived of its object. The abject is also what draws one "toward the place where meaning collapses" (Kristeva, *Powers of Horror* 2). "Topographically," one recent commentator on Kristeva's work explains, "the borderline is where the sovereignty of the sign is threatened and where something wild, something irreducible to language emerges" (Barzilai 295). Austin translates this phenomenon into a territory, calling it the Country of Lost Borders.

What all of these terms—rhythm, desire, beauty, and, indeed, wild—share is the fact that they reveal themselves to be haunted —as soon as we press our definitions far enough—by the same inexpressible emptiness. Kristeva identifies this emptiness as the *chora*, a term that appears in Plato's *Timaeus*, which she defines as the "matrix of space, nourishing, unnameable, anterior to the One, to God and, consequently, defying metaphysics" (*Kristeva Reader* 191). Translated literally from the Greek, it means "space," "room," or "region." Moreover, the *Timaeus* employs metaphors that clearly identify this baffling and obscure "space" as feminine: "the receptacle, and as it were the nurse, of all Becoming" (49a). Kristeva picks up on this and elaborates: "Indifferent to language, enigmatic and feminine, this space underlying the written is rhythmic, unfettered, irreducible to its intelligible verbal translation; it is musical, anterior to judgement" (*Kristeva Reader* 97). The *Timaeus*, true to Plato's recognition of the limits of language, goes on to say: "Wherefore, let us not speak of her that is the Mother and Receptacle of this generated world, which is perceptible by sight and all the senses, by the name of earth or air or fire or water, or any aggregates or constituents thereof: rather, if we describe her as a Kind invisible and unshaped, all-receptive, and in some most perplexing and most baffling way partaking of the intelligible, we shall describe her truly" (51a). Compare this to the *Tao Te Ching*:

> We shape clay into a pot,
> but it is the emptiness inside
> that holds whatever we want.
> (Ch. 11, Mitchell trans.)

The *chora* ("space"), like the eternal Forms, "admits of no destruction." Unlike the Platonic Forms, however, the *chora* is perceptible, albeit dimly, "without the senses by a kind of bastard reasoning, barely an object of belief; for when we regard this we dimly dream" (*Timaeus* 51a). The *chora* also bears comparison to the Buddhist concept of Bhûtatahâtâ or "suchness." As D. T. Suzuki explains it: "[Bhûtatahâtâ] marks the consummation of all our mental efforts to reach the highest principle, which unifies all possible contradictions and spontaneously directs the course of world events. In short, it is the ultimate postulate of existence. . . . it does not belong to the realm of demonstrative knowledge or sensuous experience; it is unknowable by the ordinary processes of intellection, which the natural sciences use in the formulation of general laws; and it is grasped, declare the Buddhists, only by the minds that are capable of exercising what might be called religious intuition" (Suzuki 99). What finally emerges from the discussion in the *Timaeus* is that Form (a "masculine" principle) and Space ("feminine") are the parents of Becoming. By this point, Plato has his speaker, Timaeus, dancing on the linguistic fringe; his partner is the "Unnameable," whereof we cannot speak. Plato himself is a writer of the wild.

Just as Plato has his philosopher's *chora*, so Mary Austin, a pilgrim to the wild, has hers. Here, in the Country of Lost Borders, she finds "the voiceless passion of spirit toward form that has no hope but to be broken into multiples of form, more subtly implicated, as who shall say it is not in the wild brier to be a rose, the granite mountain to be grass, the grass to be a man" (Church 197). Mary Hallock Foote, a well-known western writer of the turn of the century, after reading *The Land of Little Rain*, wrote to Austin in 1903: "For I know no one who has done or is likely to do what you are doing, dear young lady. . . . Only one of our great prose poets could write as you do of the un-writable, tell as you can the un-tellable" (Graulich 26). Austin would likely find agreement with Foucault when he writes, in *The Order of Things*, "God is perhaps not so much a region beyond knowledge as something prior to the sentences we speak; and if Western man is inseparable from him, it is not because of some invincible propensity to go beyond the frontiers of experience, but because his language ceaselessly foments him in the shadow of his laws: 'I fear indeed that we shall never rid ourselves of God, since we still believe in grammar'" (298). Mary Austin speaks of God as "the experienceable quality of the universe" (*Experiences Facing Death* 24), an ever-recharging aquifer of possibility. "God," too, is but another name for the wild.

# After Words

*Last night there was no wind, the waves were huge.*
*Rolling in, rolling out, there is a road, for whom does it pass?*
*If the place to which a hundred streams return knows*
    *contentment,*
*A little piece of cloud athwart the sky wipes out empty space.*
                            *—Ikkyū, translated by Sonja Arntzen*

Nature. God or gods. The body. The puzzling, the dark, the inexplicable, the infinite types of ambiguity, the mysterious closed in upon itself, fragmented to the eye that sees. The things before names. The emptiness. The silence. The striving. With luck, to come back with a story. This is the oldest meaning of the word *enigma*: "a story or tale."

Nature loves to hide. The booming blue grouse—*Dendragapus obscuras*—proclaiming his territory in fire-scarred red fir forest. The original ventriloquist, he can throw his voice here, there, above, below. He is a lover of trees and seldom seen. Though the pitch of his call is so low some are unable to hear it, a body passing through this forest always *feels* the voice, always knows it is there. Late April, in the upper montane forest of the Sierra Nevada. Relict banks of snow melting into rich duff, millions of fir seeds scattering and scattered, each bursting with a tiny red root, desiring earth. Few will survive this exuberance. Orgy of moisture followed by orgy of light. But still, the snowpack is below "normal." Dust is inevitable. Some trees will fall to native beetles engraving their trace in xylem and phloem. Ravishing. Insects, too, have their orgy. As do woodpeckers.

The signature of all things. The book of nature. Not just a tired metaphor, but the fundamental way in which the world was once known, may still be known. Somewhere along the way, we confused a process with a literary trope, substituted manner for action, and set ourselves up in paddocks. The institutions. Here we make our stands, view the spectacle, and write our own books. We no longer read the weather but the weather report. Nevertheless, the older world still haunts our words. It's the "it" when we say: "It's raining."

# Works Cited

Adams, Henry. *The Education of Henry Adams.* Boston: Houghton Mifflin, 1973 (1918).

Adams, Stephen, and Donald Ross, Jr. *Revising Mythologies: The Composition of Thoreau's Major Works.* Charlottesville: University Press of Virginia, 1988.

Aristotle. *Introduction to Aristotle.* New York: Modern Library, 1947.

———. *The Rhetoric of Aristotle,* trans. Lane Cooper. New York: Meredith, 1932.

Austin, Mary. *Earth Horizon.* Boston: Houghton Mifflin, 1932.

———. *Experiences Facing Death.* Indianapolis: Bobbs-Merrill, 1931.

———. *California, Land of the Sun.* New York: Macmillan, 1914.

———. "Lost Garden." Unpublished ms., Mary Hunter Austin Collection. Henry E. Huntington Library, San Marino, California.

———. "Lost Others." Unpublished ms., Mary Hunter Austin Collection. Henry E. Huntington Library, San Marino, California.

———. "Sex in American Literature." *The Bookman* 57 (June 1923): 385–93.

———. *Stories from the Country of Lost Borders,* ed. Marjorie Pryse. New Brunswick: Rutgers University Press, 1987.

———. "Woman Alone." *The Nation* 124 (March 2, 1927): 228–30.

Badé, William Frederic. *The Life and Letters of John Muir.* 2 vols. Boston and New York: Houghton Mifflin, 1924.

Barthes, Roland. *A Lover's Discourse.* New York: Farrar, Straus and Giroux, 1978.

Barzilai, Shuli. "Borders of Language: Kristeva's Critique of Lacan." *PMLA* 106, no. 2 (March 1991): 294–305.

Bennett, Paula. *Emily Dickinson: Woman Poet.* Iowa City: University of Iowa Press, 1990.

Bercovitch, Sacvan. *The American Puritan Imagination.* Cambridge: Cambridge University Press, 1974.

Bunyan, John. *The Pilgrim's Progress.* New York: New American Library, 1981.

Callicott, J. Baird, and Roger T. Ames. *Nature in Asian Traditions of Thought: Essays in Environmental Philosophy*. Albany: State University of New York Press, 1989.

Cameron, Sharon. *Writing Nature: Henry Thoreau's Journal*. Chicago: University of Chicago Press, 1988.

Carson, Anne. *Eros the Bittersweet*. Princeton: Princeton University Press, 1986.

Church, Peggy Pond. *Wind's Trail: The Early Life of Mary Austin*. Santa Fe: Museum of New Mexico Press, 1990.

Cobb, Edith. *The Ecology of Imagination in Childhood*. New York: Columbia University Press, 1977.

Cohen, Michael. *The Pathless Way: John Muir and the American Wilderness*. Madison: University of Wisconsin Press, 1984.

Colby, William E., ed. *John Muir's Studies in the Sierra*. San Francisco: Sierra Club Books, 1960 (1949).

de Man, Paul. *Blindness and Insight*. Revised ed. Minneapolis: University of Minnesota Press, 1983 (1971).

Deleuze, Gilles, and Felix Guattari. *Anti-Oedipus*. trans. Robert Hurley, Mark Seem, and Helen R. Lane. New York: Viking, 1977.

Devall, Bill, and George Sessions. *Deep Ecology*. Salt Lake City: Peregrine Smith, 1985.

Dickinson, Emily. *The Complete Poems of Emily Dickinson*, ed. Thomas H. Johnson. Boston: Little, Brown and Company, 1960.

Dōgen. *Moon in a Dewdrop: Writings of Zen Master Dōgen*, ed. Kazuaki Tanahashi. San Francisco: North Point, 1985.

Ehrlich, Gretel. *The Solace of Open Spaces*. New York: Viking Penguin, 1985.

Emerson, Ralph Waldo. *The Selected Writings of Ralph Waldo Emerson*, ed. Brooks Atkinson. New York: Modern Library, 1968.

Engberg, Robert. *John Muir: Summering in the Sierra*. Madison: University of Wisconsin Press, 1984.

Engberg, Robert, and Donald Wesling, eds. *John Muir: To Yosemite and Beyond: Writings from the Years 1863 to 1875*. Madison: University of Wisconsin Press, 1980.

Enyeart, James L. *Edward Weston's California Landscapes*. Boston: Little, Brown and Company, 1984.

Farquhar, Francis. *History of the Sierra Nevada*. Berkeley: University of California Press, 1966.

Fink, Augusta. *I-Mary: A Biography of Mary Austin*. Tucson: University of Arizona Press, 1983.

Fish, Stanley. *Self-Consuming Artifacts: The Experience of Seventeenth-Century Literature*. Berkeley: University of California Press, 1972.

Foucault, Michel. *The Order of Things.* New York: Vintage, 1973.

———. *Politics, Philosophy, Culture: Interviews and Other Writings, 1977–1984.* New York and London: Routledge, 1988.

———. *Power/Knowledge: Selected Interviews and Other Writings, 1972–1977.* New York: Pantheon Books, 1980.

Fox, Stephen. *The American Conservation Movement: John Muir and His Legacy.* Madison: University of Wisconsin Press, 1985 (1981).

Freud, Sigmund. *Civilization and Its Discontents.* New York: Norton, 1961.

———. *General Psychological Theory.* New York: Collier, 1963.

Golemba, Henry. *Thoreau's Wild Rhetoric.* New York: New York University Press, 1990.

Gould, Stephen J. "Darwinism and the Expansion of Evolutionary Theory." *Science* 216 (23 April 1982): 380–87.

Graulich, Melody, ed. *Western Trails: A Collection of Stories by Mary Austin.* Reno and Las Vegas: University of Nevada Press, 1987.

Graves, Robert. *The White Goddess: A Historical Grammar of Poetic Myth.* New York: Farrar, Straus and Giroux, 1966.

Hague, James D., ed. *Clarence King Memoirs.* New York: G. P. Putnam and Sons, for the King Memorial Committee of the Century Association, 1904.

Hart, James D., ed. *My First Publication.* San Francisco: Book Club of California, 1961.

Heilbrun, Carolyn. *Writing a Woman's Life.* New York: Ballantine, 1988.

Houghland, Willard, ed. *Mary Austin: A Memorial.* Santa Fe: Laboratory of Anthropology, 1944.

Ikkyū. *Ikkyū and the Crazy Cloud Anthology,* trans. Sonja Arntzen. Tokyo: University of Tokyo Press, 1986.

Johnson, Barbara. *A World of Difference.* Baltimore: Johns Hopkins University Press, 1987.

Kimes, William and Maymie. *John Muir: A Reading Bibliography.* Fresno: Panorama West Books, 1986.

King, Clarence. "The Age of the Earth." *American Journal of Science* 45 (January 1893): 1–20.

———. "Artium Magister." *North American Review* 147 (October 1888): 369–84.

———. "Catastrophism and Evolution." *American Naturalist* 11 (August 1877): 449–70.

———. Clarence King Papers. Henry E. Huntington Library, San Marino, California.

———. "The Education of the Future." *Forum* 13 (March 1892): 20–33.

————. *Mountaineering in the Sierra Nevada.* 4th ed. Boston: James R. Os-
good and Company, 1874 (1872).

————. *Mountaineering in the Sierra Nevada,* ed. Francis Farquhar. New
York: W. W. Norton and Company, 1935 (1872).

————. *Systematic Geology.* Washington, D.C.: U.S. Government Print-
ing Office, 1878.

Kristeva, Julia. *The Kristeva Reader,* ed. Toril Moi. New York: Columbia
University Press, 1986.

————. *The Powers of Horror: An Essay on Abjection.* New York: Columbia University Press, 1982.

————. *Tales of Love.* New York: Columbia University Press, 1987.

Lapidus, Dorothy F. *Dictionary of Geology and Geophysics.* New York:
Facts on File, 1987.

Lawrence, D. H. *Psychoanalysis and the Unconscious* and *Fantasia and the
Unconscious.* New York: Viking, 1960.

Lebeaux, Richard. *Thoreau's Seasons.* Amherst: University of Massachusetts Press, 1984.

Lévi-Strauss, Claude. *The Savage Mind.* Chicago: University of Chicago
Press, 1966.

Marx, Leo. *The Machine in the Garden: Technology and the Pastoral Ideal in
America.* New York: Oxford University Press, 1964.

Mitchell, Stephen, trans. *Tao Te Ching.* New York: Harper and Row, 1988.

Muir, John. "A Flood-Storm in the Sierra." *The Overland Monthly* 14, no.
6 (1875): 489–96.

————. "A Geologist's Winter Walk." *The Overland Monthly* 10, no. 4
(1873): 355–58.

————. "The Humming-Bird of the California Water-Falls." *Scribner's
Monthly* 15, no. 4 (1878): 545–54.

————. "In the Heart of the California Alps." *Scribner's Monthly* 20, no.
3 (1880): 345–52.

————. *John of the Mountains: The Unpublished Journals of John Muir,* ed.
Linnie Marsh Wolfe. Madison. University of Wisconsin Press, 1979
(1938).

————. *Letters to a Friend: Written to Mrs. Ezra S. Carr, 1866–1879.*
Dunwoody, Georgia: Norman S. Berg Publisher, 1973.

————. *The Mountains of California.* Reprint, 1st ed. Berkeley: Ten Speed
Press, n. d. [1894].

————. *My First Summer in the Sierra,* ed. Gretel Ehrlich. New York:
Viking Penguin, 1987.

————. *Steep Trails,* ed. William Frederic Badé. Boston and New York:
Houghton Mifflin, 1918.

————. *A Thousand-Mile Walk to the Gulf.* Boston: Houghton Mifflin, 1916.

————. "Twenty Hill Hollow." *The Overland Monthly* 9, no. 1 (1872): 80–86.

————. "A Wind Storm in the Forests of the Yuba." *Scribner's Monthly* 17, no. 1 (1878): 55–59.

————. "Yosemite Valley in Flood." *The Overland Monthly* 8, no. 4 (1872): 347–50.

Muir, John, ed. *Picturesque California and the Region West of the Rocky Mountains from Alaska to Mexico.* 2 vols. San Francisco: J. Dewing, 1888.

Nietzsche, Friedrich. *Beyond Good and Evil,* trans. Walter Kaufmann. New York: Vintage, 1966.

————. *The Gay Science,* trans. Walter Kaufmann. New York: Vintage, 1974.

———. *Untimely Meditations,* trans. R. J. Hollingdale. Cambridge: Cambridge University Press, 1983.

Olson, Charles. *Call Me Ishmael.* San Francisco: City Lights Books, 1947.

Oppen, George. *Collected Poems.* New York: New Directions, 1975.

Petrarch. *Letters from Petrarch,* trans. Morris Bishop. Bloomington: Indiana University Press, 1966.

Plato. *The Collected Dialogues,* ed. Edith Hamilton and Huntington Cairns. Princeton: Princeton University Press, 1961.

————. *Timeaus: With an English Translation,* trans. R. G. Bury. Cambridge: Harvard University Press, 1952 (1929).

*Resource Conservation Glossary.* Ankeny, Iowa: Soil Conservation Society of America, 1982.

Rexroth, Kenneth. "Camping in the Western Mountains." Unpublished ms. Special Collections, Doheny Library, University of Southern California.

Rilke, Rainer Maria. *The Selected Poetry of Rainer Maria Rilke,* ed. and trans. Stephen Mitchell. New York: Random House, 1982.

Rusho, W. L. *Everett Ruess: Vagabond for Beauty.* Salt Lake City: Peregrine Smith, 1983.

St. Armand, Barton Levy. "Veiled Ladies: Dickinson, Bettine, and Transcendental Mediumship." In *Studies in the American Renaissance,* ed. Joel Myerson. Charlottesville: University Press of Virginia, 1987.

Smith, Michael L. *Pacific Visions: California Scientists and the Environment, 1850–1915.* New Haven: Yale University Press, 1987.

Snyder, Gary. *The Practice of the Wild.* San Francisco: North Point, 1990.

Spinoza, Baruch. *The Collected Works of Spinoza,* ed. and trans. Edwin

Curley. Vol. 1. Princeton: Princeton University Press, 1985.

Stegner, Wallace. *Beyond the Hundredth Meridian*. Boston: Houghton Mifflin, 1954.

———. *The American West as Living Space*. Ann Arbor: University of Michigan Press, 1987.

Stineman, Esther. *Mary Austin: Song of a Maverick*. New Haven: Yale University Press, 1989.

Stoller, Leo. *After Walden*. Palo Alto: Stanford University Press, 1957.

Suzuki, D. T. *Outlines of Mahayana Buddhism*. New York: Schocken Books, 1963.

Thoreau, Henry D. *The Correspondence of Henry David Thoreau*, ed. Walter Harding and Carl Bode. New York: New York University Press, 1958.

———. *The Journal of Henry David Thoreau*, ed. Bradford Torrey and Francis H. Allen. 14 vols. Boston: Houghton Mifflin, 1906.

———. *The Maine Woods*. Princeton: Princeton University Press, 1972.

———. *The Variorum Walden*, ed. Walter Harding. New York: Twayne, 1962.

———. "Walking." *The Atlantic Monthly* 9, no. 56 (June 1862): 657–74.

———. *A Week on the Concord and Merrimack Rivers*. Princeton: Princeton University Press, 1983.

Tobias, Michael. *Deep Ecology*. San Diego: Avant Books, 1985.

Turner, Frederick. *Rediscovering America: John Muir in His Time and Ours*. New York: Viking, 1985.

Turner, Victor and Edith. *Image and Pilgrimage in Christian Culture*. New York: Columbia University Press, 1978.

van Gennep, Arnold. *The Rites of Passage*. Chicago: University of Chicago Press, 1960.

Watson, Burton, trans. *Chuang Tzu*. New York: Columbia University Press, 1964.

Watts, Alan. *Tao: The Watercourse Way*. New York: Pantheon Books, 1975.

Welch, Lew. *Ring of Bone: Collected Poems, 1950–1971*. Bolinas: Grey Fox Press, 1979.

Welter, Barbara. *Dimity Convictions: The American Woman in the Nineteenth Century*. Athens: Ohio University Press, 1976.

Wilbur, J. B. and H. J. Allen, eds. *The Worlds of the Early Greek Philosophers*. Buffalo: Prometheus Books, 1979.

Wild, Peter. *Clarence King*. Boise: Boise State University Western Writers Series (no. 48), 1981.

Wilkins, Thurman. *Clarence King: A Biography.* Rev. and enlarged ed. Albuquerque: University of New Mexico Press, 1988 (1958).

Wolfe, Linnie Marsh. *Son of the Wilderness: The Life of John Muir.* Madison: University of Wisconsin Press, 1979.

# Index

Abjection, 151
Adams, Henry, 94, 107, 109
Agassiz, Louis, 92
Ambivalence, 94–96
American Pre-Raphaelites, 92
Anthropology, 13
Aristotle, 10–11, 34, 35
Art, 15–16, 20, 64–65
*The Atlantic Monthly*, 23
Austin, Mary Hunter
  experiential quality of the wild, 127–38
  as reluctant pilgrim, 123–26
  rhythm as theme in later writing, 149–53
  wild and nature writing, 138–49
Austin, Stafford, 144
Autobiography, 139

Bade, William Frederick, 54n.6
Barthes, Roland, 7
Beauty, 10
Bennett, Paula, 135
Bercovitch, Sacvan, 114
Bhûtatahâtâ, 152–53
Black, A. G., 71
Blake, William, 35
Body, 43, 45, 63
Boundaries, 32, 140–41
Brewer, William, 92, 117, 118
Brownsville, California, 74–75
Buddhism
  concept of Bhûtatahâtâ, 152–53
  experience of liminality, 98
  guides and pilgrimages, 3

Japanese tradition and pilgrimages, 53
as method of perception, 134
translation from common sense to pure mind, 41
Bunyan, John, x, xii, 52

Cameron, Sharon, 25n.1
Canons, literary, xii
Carr, Jeanne, 50, 60–61, 66, 72
Carson, Anne, 32, 33
Catastrophism, 110–15
Cathexis, 94
Chopin, Kate, 62n.11
*Chora*, 151–53
Church, Peggy Pond, 129
Civil War, 51, 92
Cohen, Michael, 54n.6
Common sense, 43n.7
Communism, 6
Community, 4–5, 6–7, 14
Cotter, Dick, 115
Creation myth, 148–49
Cult of true womanhood. *See* Womanhood, cult of true

Decisiveness, 13
Deep ecology, 76–78. *See also* Ecology
Desert, 137–38, 138–39
Desire. *See also* Love
  Austin and loss, 129
  Austin and the wild, 150–51
  author's use of term, xi
  King and scientific discourse, 120
  Muir and nature writing, 56–57, 58–59, 61–70, 81